In Christ Jesus

General Editor

Rev. Gerard P. Weber

Consulting Editors

Rev. James J. Killgallon
Sr. M. Michael O'Shaughnessy, O.P.

BENZIGER PUBLISHING COMPANY

Encino, California

Photographs

Page
20 NASA
21 © Dennis Stock/Magnum
62 © Scala/EPA
65 © Eric Lessing/Magnum
88 © Eric Lessing/Magnum
116 © Scala/EPA
119 © Owen Franken/Stock Boston
142 © Shelly Grossman/Woodfin Camp
 & Associates
176 U.P.I.
178 U.P.I.
197 © Bill Strode/Woodfin Camp
 & Associates
208 © Jeffrey Foxx/Woodfin Camp
 & Associates
209 John Maher
216 © Tim Eagan/Woodfin Camp
 & Associates
219 © W. McNamar/Woodfin Camp
 & Associates

Other Photographs

B. Baker
CARE
Dwight Cendroski
Dan DeWilde
Mimi Forsyth
Tony Freeman
William Heineken
Stephen McBrady
NCN
Robert Pacheco
Nick Pavlov
Jerome Riordan
Hugh Rogers
J. Schaeffer
Rick Smolan
David Strickler
Bob Taylor
United Nations

Illustrations

Julie Downing
Christa Kieffer
Francis Livingstone
Terrence Meagher
James McConnell
Heather Preston

Nihil Obstat:
Msgr. John K. Clarke
Censor Deputatus

Imprimatur:
+ Timothy Cardinal Manning
Archbishop of Los Angeles
March 30, 1982

The nihil obstat and imprimatur are official declarations that a book or pamphlet is free of doctrinal or moral error. No implication is contained therein that those who have granted the nihil obstat and imprimatur agree with the contents, opinions, or statements expressed.

Benziger Publishing Company
17337 Ventura Boulevard
Encino, California 91316
Collier Macmillan Canada, Ltd.

Printed in the United States
ISBN 0-02-653810-5 (Student)
ISBN 0-02-653820-2 (TE/School)
ISBN 0-02-653830-X (TE/CCD)

4 5 6 7 8 9   86 85

Contents

Handbook

See what love the Father has bestowed on us in letting us be called children of God! Yet that is what we are. The reason the world does not recognize us is that it never recognized the Son. Dearly beloved, we are God's children now; what we shall later be has not yet come to light. We know that when it comes to light, we shall be like Him, for we shall see Him as He is.

(1 John 3:1–2)

PART ONE

Children of God

1

Someone Special

In This Chapter

You will see how you try to answer the question, "Who am I?"

You will learn that Jesus came to remind you just how special you are.

You will rediscover your own specialness.

Who Am I?

he Natural Science Museum of the Smithsonian Institute in Washington, D.C., has on exhibit a very special computer. This computer can change the characteristics of a human face displayed on a television screen. By using the computer, an operator can change the nose, lengthen the chin, shift the eyes, or enlarge the ears.

The device was developed to help criminal investigators identify suspects. Victims or witnesses in criminal cases can use the machine to give as accurate a description as possible of the person who committed an offense. The collection of features, scars, hairline, coloring, and the like will assist the police in answering the question, "Who is it?"

People stand in line at the museum to get a chance to play with this computer. There is something very fascinating about being able to change a face—to

create an identity. It is almost as if the people working the machine are asking the question, "Who am I,
and who would I be if I changed?"

People are different. People come in different sizes,
shapes, and colors. Unless you are an identical twin,
there is no one on earth who looks exactly like you.
Nobody anywhere has exactly the same talents, likes,
looks, intelligence, feelings, or personality that you
have. All of those things are part of the recipe which
has made you the person you are. Yet, if you are like
most people, there are things about yourself you
would like to change.

Use the format below to identify yourself as you
see yourself today. Briefly describe yourself. Then,
describe what you might want to change about yourself. Finally, describe why you want to change.

Quality	Description	Change	Reason
1. Appearance			
2. Intelligence			
3. Talent			
4. Emotions			
5. Personality			

Questions

1. Were most of your descriptions of yourself positive or negative? Why?
2. Which quality was the hardest for you to describe? Why?
3. How many of your reasons for changing involved a comparison between yourself and another person? Why did you make the comparison?

Activities

1. Each person in the class can write a brief description of him or herself. Put all the descriptions together in a box. Draw descriptions from the box one at a time. Let the class guess who is being described.
2. Look through magazines or watch television commercials to discover what is considered to be the ideal image of a person. Discuss your discoveries in class.

Christian Identity

Growing up is a process of discovery. Perhaps the biggest discovery you can make is to find out who you are. Of all the billions of different people in the world, you are unique. There is nobody just like you. This year, you will be discovering more about yourself and the people who share the Catholic Faith. You are going to be learning how you—a unique human being—are part of the great Family of the followers of Jesus. You will be learning this in three ways.

1. You will discover more about yourself—how you feel and how you act.
2. You will discover more about yourself as a follower of Jesus.
3. You will discover how you and the other members of the Christian Family take care of one another.

Making Comparisons

One way people have of discovering who they are is comparing themselves to others. Liz is the smartest person in class. Frank is the fastest person on the team. Alex wears good clothes. Edward's clothes are better. Dolly's family has a better car than Tom's has. Loren is the best-looking person in the room. Comparisons go on and on.

Comparisons can be helpful. They give you a sense of who you are in relation to others. More often than not, however, comparisons are dangerous. There are traps in comparing. First of all, comparisons offer the trap of competition. People can be so busy trying to be better, prettier, faster, or smarter that they never discover who they really are. The question, "Who am I?" becomes "How can I get ahead of others?"

Secondly, comparisons offer the trap of false standards to give a person identity. The question, "Who am I?" becomes "What do I have?" or "How do I look?" or "Where do I live?" or "Who are my friends?"

Thirdly, comparisons can lead to the trap of discouragement. It is not too difficult to find someone more talented, richer, more famous, smarter, or better looking. In this kind of discouraging atmosphere, the question, "Who am I?" becomes "I wish I were different!"

Thousands of years ago, your ancestors, the people of Israel, had trouble with comparisons. When God called Abraham to be the father of a great nation, He started the process of helping the people of Israel recognize themselves as the People of God.

> You are a people sacred to the Lord your God; He has chosen you from all the nations on the face of the earth to be a people peculiarly His own. It was not because you are the largest of all nations that the Lord set His heart on you and chose you, for you are really the smallest of all nations. It was because the Lord loved you.

(Deuteronomy 7:6–8)

Before long, the Israelites were comparing themselves to others, competing with others, trying to be better than their neighbors, and wishing they were different. The Egyptians had more culture. The Babylonians were richer. The Sumerians had a more beautiful land. The Edomites did not have such difficult laws to follow. The Persians were strong and powerful. And finally, the Romans had the greatest armies in the world.

God constantly reminded the Israelites that they were special because He called and loved them. God even sent a guide to help them avoid the traps of comparisons. God sent His only Son, Jesus, into the world to remind people that they were important. Jesus had the *mission* to remind people that they were made good and special, that they were loved and trusted by God, and that they had their own ways of revealing God to others.

Mission A task a person is sent to accomplish. The mission of Jesus was to save the world from sin and death, and to announce the kingdom of God. The mission of baptized Christians is to continue the work of Jesus.

VIPs

Everyone has daydreams of being rich and famous or of being treated like a very important person. Maybe in your daydream, you step out of a big limousine. All around are cheering crowds. You look up and see your name in lights. You walk down a long red carpet. Lights, reporters, cameras, and tape recorders are everywhere. Everyone is reaching out to you because you are so special—so great.

You are a VIP. No one is following you around with microphones and cameras. But if someone did, he or she would soon discover that you are the only one of your kind. There is no one like you. The message of Jesus to each one of His followers underlines just how important each person is.

But because you need to be told how special you are, Jesus brought a message of love. "You are the salt of the earth," He said. "You are the light of the world." He went on to say,

> "Look at the birds in the sky. They do not sow or reap, they gather nothing into barns; yet your heavenly Father feeds them. Are not you more important than they? Which of you by worrying can add a moment to your life-span? As for clothes, why be concerned? Learn a lesson from the way the wild flowers grow. They do not work; they do not spin. Yet I assure you, not even Solomon in all his splendor was arrayed like one of these. If God can clothe in such splendor the grass of the field, which blooms today and is thrown on the fire tomorrow, will He not provide much more for you."
>
> *(Matthew 6:26–31)*

Jesus also showed how much He trusted His followers. He *revealed* Himself to them. He left them the treasure of His innermost thoughts. Jesus knew how important and special you feel when someone trusts you enough to let you come very close.

Reveal To make something known. God's plans for caring for His People were revealed to Abraham, Moses, and the prophets. Jesus reveals God the Father in Person.

"I am the vine, you are the branches. . . .
As the Father has loved Me,
so I have loved you.
Live on in My love. . . .
You are My friends
if you do what I command you.
I no longer speak of you as servants,
for a servant does not know what the master
    is about.
Instead, I call you friends,
since I have made known to you all that I heard
    from my Father.
It was not you who chose Me,
it was I who chose you."

(John 15:5–16)

Finally, Jesus showed how important each person is by trusting each to share God's message with others. He trusted that His followers would do their job by loving and caring for all the VIPs in the world.

"I give you a new commandment:
Love one another.
Such as My love has been for you,
So must your love be for each other.
This is how all will know you for My disciples:
your love for one another."

(John 13:34–35)

Your Own Specialness

What Jesus was saying to His disciples two thousand years ago, He is still saying today. Within the Church, Jesus reminds everyone of his or her own specialness. "You are good—you have My life. You can be trusted with My love. You can do the job I have given you to do!"

Throughout this book, you will be discovering your Christian identity. You will discover how special you are. You will learn how to act and to behave in order to show your specialness. You will also discover ways to celebrate and to share your specialness. Most of all, you will be answering the question, "Who am I?" The answer may surprise you and make you proud and happy to say, "I am a very important person—a friend and follower of Jesus."

Questions

1. In what three ways can you discover your Christian identity?
2. In what three ways did Jesus show His disciples how special they were?
3. What are the dangers of making comparisons?
4. Recall a time when someone trusted you. How did this trust make you feel? What did this trust teach you about yourself?

Activity

Describe a time when you compared yourself with someone else. Why did you make each comparison? How did each comparison make you feel? What did each comparison teach you about yourself? Did you fall into any of the traps mentioned in this section? Discuss your answers in small groups.

Who Do You Think You Are?

ne of the first steps in discovering your Christian identity is to get a pretty good picture of yourself: (1) what you can and cannot do, (2) how well you do, and (3) how proud you are of what you do. So, you are invited to make some comparisons now. Try to avoid the three big traps. Start with the idea that God has made you someone special.

1. Name one thing you can do better than others do.

   _____

   How do you feel when you do that thing better than someone else?

   _____

   How do you treat people who do not do something as well as you do?

   _____

2. Name one thing you can do about as well as others do.

   _____

   How do you feel when you seem to be the same as others?

   _____

   How do you treat people of about equal ability?

   _____

3. Name one thing you do not do as well as others.

   _____

   How do you feel when you do not do as well as others?

   _____

   How do you treat people who do something better than you do?

   _____

4. In one sentence, give an honest picture of yourself.

   _____

Review

Circle the T if the statement is true. Circle the F if the statement is false.

1. It is very important for a person to know him or herself.   T   F

2. You should never compare yourself to others.   T   F

3. Jesus showed how important people were by trusting them.   T   F

4. The Israelites never compared themselves with others.   T   F

5. Christians are not very important people.   T   F

Projects

1. Create a chart of the traps people can fall into when they are comparing themselves with others. On the chart, show the three major traps. Then, give examples of how a person falls into each trap. Finally, give examples of how a follower of Jesus can avoid the traps. Take your chart home to share it with your family.

2. Create a short prayer service to celebrate the fact that each person is a VIP. Before the prayer service, exchange names. During the service, each person must tell the person whose name he or she has drawn why that person is a VIP. Page 284 of your Handbook will help you. You may want to use the prayer service as the opening of the next class.

Prayer

Praise be the God and Father of our Lord Jesus Christ, who has given us in Christ every spiritual blessing in the heavens! God chose us in Christ before the world began, to be holy and blameless in His sight, to be full of love. He likewise called us through Christ Jesus to be His adopted children.

(Ephesians 1:3–5)

2
Loved by God

In This Chapter

*You will discover that you have
a special place in creation.*

*You will see that God has given
you the whole universe as a gift.*

*You will review how you can
share God's love with others.*

Feeling Great, Feeling Small

Sometimes it is very hard to believe that you are important. When you look around you, sometimes you feel big, and at other times you feel pretty small. When you feel big, you might feel important. When you feel small, you might feel very unimportant.

Consider some statistics. In 1981, the average male on this planet had a height of 5' 10", weighed 167 lb., and had a 38¾" chest, a 31¾" waist, and 37¾" hips. The average female was 5' 3¾" tall, weighed 135 lb., and measured 35½" at the bust, and had a 29¼" waist and 38" hips. Based on comparisons of mass, a human body equals 7.29×10^{22} viruses, 7.29×10^{15} bacteria, 1×10^{14} cells, 1.46×10^{10} parasitic wasps, or 7.29×10^{5} house spiders. Based on comparisons of weight, you will find that a human body equals 37,029 hummingbirds, 134.6 rats, 105 guinea pigs, 27 ringtail monkeys, 20 rabbits, 19.3 chickens, 9.6 cats, or 5.9 porcupines. From the perspective of any one of these smaller creatures, the human being is a pretty big deal.

When you begin to look at other animals, plants, or the galaxy, the size of the human person begins to shrink astronomically. Consider that 37,000 people can stand on an American football field, and more than 51,000 people can fit on a soccer field.

Based on comparisons of mass, the human person becomes no more than a fleck of dust. The mass of a polar bear equals the mass of 4.4 persons. An African elephant equals the weight of 86 people. A blue whale equals the weight of 1,900 people (the whole population of Mosinee, Wisconsin). The mass of the earth equals that of 8.2×10^{22} people. The total mass of the planets in our solar system equals 3.7×10^{25} people. The sun equals 2.7×10^{28} people, and the total

mass of the galaxy equals 3×10^{39} people. If you worked out those numbers, there would not be room in your classroom for all the zeroes.

So, there you are—smack in the middle of creation. You are made up of billions and billions of atoms and molecules. Yet, if you spent the rest of your life traveling, you could not reach the closest star. In the reality of God's creation, you are both very great and very small.

Questions

1. In comparison to viruses, bacteria, and many insects, how do you feel about being so big?
2. In comparison to a blue whale, the sun, or the galaxy, how do you feel about being so small?
3. How can the fact that you are alive be a sign of God's love for you?

Activities

1. Read Psalm 8 and then share some thoughts about the place of human beings in the universe. Do this as a poem, short essay, song, slide show, or drawing.
2. Read Genesis 2:18–23. In small groups, discuss the relationship of human beings to (a) nature, (b) other people, and (c) technology. What responsibilities do people have in each of these relationships?

The Gift of Creation

Two little words tell about the excitement you feel when you peel back the wrappings and tissue, and say, "For me?" You know the excitement of receiving a present. You know, too, just how important receiving presents can make you feel. Somebody cared enough to give you something that you did not earn.

One of the best presents you have ever received comes wrapped in grass and water and snow. It has rivers and streams for ribbons. It is decorated with billions of living creatures—flowers, trees, fish, birds, animals. Looking out your window, running down a country path, or walking down a busy street, you could look at all the excitement of the world and say, "For me?" And the answer would be yes!

When you really care about someone, it seems very natural to give a gift. Because God cares so much for you, it is very natural for Him to give you gifts, too.

Then God said: "Let us make people in our image, after our likeness. Let them have dominion over the fish of the sea, the birds of the air, and the cattle, and over all the wild animals and all the creatures that crawl on the ground."

(Genesis 1:26)

If you have ever watched a very small child at a birthday party, you understand a little better how beautiful a gift is creation. The young toddler stands in the midst of balloons and streamers. Her eyes are wide with wonder. She wants to grab everything at once. She rips open presents and squeals with happiness. She runs with her friends to the cake and ice cream. Everything is wonderful. It is as if the whole world has hatched a plot to make the youngster happy.

God has hatched a plot to make you happy. You are alive to be happy. God created you because of His great love for you. He wants you and every person on earth to be happy—now and forever. God's plan for you is that you recognize and love Him, that you be happy in His love, and that you share His love.

You Are No Accident

Part of God's plot to make you happy was to show you—in person—just how much you are loved. Thousands of years ago, people looked at the warmth of their campfires and saw the wonder of the flames. They *worshiped* the fire because of the good it brought them. Some people prayed to the sun because they saw the wonder the sun brought to the day, to their crops, to the purple mountaintops. Some people worshiped water because they lived in dry climates where water was very precious and important.

For thousands of years, people thought that gods were hiding in creation—gods that held the power of

Worship To pray, to celebrate liturgy, and to honor God. When you participate at Mass or do a kind deed because you love God, you are worshiping Him.

life and death, happiness or despair over the people. When the time was right, God let Himself be recognized as the one true God, the God who loves the people He has made. He asked people to remember Him and be faithful to Him. He gave these people a land to call their very own—the land of Israel.

But God knew that you might need more to see just how much He loves you. So, when the time was right again, God stepped into the beautiful world He had made. He became a human person in Jesus, His Son.

Jesus lived in only one small corner of God's beautiful world. He probably never traveled more than two hundred miles from the spot where He was born. But in the few short years Jesus lived on earth, He showed that God's love was real. Wherever He went, Jesus told good news to the poor. He healed the sick. He comforted the people who were sad. He gave sight to the blind. He made crippled people walk. He told stories about God the Father—how His rule was like a treasure hidden in a field, or yeast in flour, or like a mustard seed.

> "Ask, and you will receive. Seek, and you will find. Knock, and it will be opened to you. For the one who asks, receives. The one who seeks, finds. The one who knocks, enters. Would one of you hand your son a stone when he asks for a loaf of bread, or a poisonous snake when he asks for a fish? If you know how to give your children what is good, how much more will your heavenly Father give good things to anyone who asks Him!"
>
> *(Matthew 7:7–11)*

The people who watched and listened to Jesus began to see how loved they were. They talked about what Jesus said and did. They began to change. They no longer felt lonely or afraid. They no longer felt small and unimportant. They began to greet one another like brothers and sisters because they knew that each of them was loved by God.

One day, Jesus was talking to His friends and disciples. All of a sudden, He stopped. A big smile came over His face. He looked up to the sky. His friends wondered just what was happening. Jesus prayed,

"I offer You praise, O Father, Lord of heaven and earth, because what You have hidden from the learned and clever, You have revealed to the merest children...." Turning to His disciples, He said to them: "Blest are the eyes that see what you see. I tell you, many prophets and kings wished to see what you see but did not see it, and to hear what you hear but did not hear it."

(Luke 10:21, 23–24)

Acting Loved

Jesus wanted His disciples to realize that God's love is a gift that no one can earn. So, He told them a story about a certain farmer who needed people to work in his vineyard. Early in the morning, the man went into the town and hired several workers and

promised them a day's wages. About the middle of the morning, the farmer went out and found more workers. He went out at noon and hired a few more. Late in the afternoon, he hired some more workers. When the sun was setting, the workers lined up to get their pay. The farmer gave the men who had worked just one hour a whole day's wages. He did the same for those who were hired at noon. When the workers who had worked the whole day came to the front of the line, they thought they would receive more. But they got a day's pay, too. They complained. But the farmer said, "I did you no injustice. You agreed to work for a day's pay. Are you angry because I am generous?" *(Matthew 20:1–16)*.

Nobody can earn the gift of being alive. Nobody can earn the beauties of creation. There is no contest you can enter in which the first prize is a month's supply of God's love. Instead, God has offered you a lifetime supply of His love as a gift—no charge and no strings attached. All you have to do is accept the gift.

You accept the gift when you recognize in the beauties of sunsets and snowstorms the presence of God. You accept the gift when you thank God for letting you be alive in the world. You accept the gift when you act like someone who is loved by God— someone who is proud and happy to be a follower of His Son, Jesus. Most of all, you accept the great gift your loving Father has given you by sharing the gift with others—by helping others feel loved and cared for.

Questions

1. What does it mean that creation is a gift from God? How is it a gift *for you?*
2. What are two ways Jesus taught His disciples about the Father's love?
3. What are three ways you can act like you are loved by God?

Activity

Each student in the class can make one symbol that tells about how the gift of creation is the sign of God's love. Draw the symbols and cut them out. Then, either string the symbols together or hang them on a bulletin board. Each person should have the chance to explain his or her symbol.

Signs of God's Love

Sometimes it is very helpful to put down on paper just how much you are loved and cared for. Copy the chart below. The first four questions are private—you need not share them with anyone. Share the last four questions with the class as a whole or in small groups. Remember that these questions are helping you answer the big question, "Who am I?"

Questions	Responses
1. What is one way God has shown His love for you?	
2. Name two people who love you.	
3. How do you know that they love you?	
4. How does their love for you make you feel?	
5. How do you know when you are loved?	
6. What is one way for you to accept the gift of God's love?	
7. What is one way for you to show God's love to others?	
8. What is your favorite reminder of God's love?	

Review

1. How do the statistics given in the beginning of this chapter remind you that you are loved by God?

2. In what ways is creation a gift?

3. What is the lesson of the story of the workers in the vineyard?

4. List four ways to accept God's gift of love.

Projects

1. In small groups, make a list of obstacles to recognizing God's love in the gift of creation. Some of these obstacles may be internal—people do not believe they are loved by God. Some of these obstacles may be external—hunger, poverty, or other world problems. Try to list at least ten obstacles. When the group has agreed on a list, pick one of the obstacles mentioned and discuss a possible remedy.

2. Prepare one thing you can do at home to act like a person who is loved by God. You may want to discuss this in small groups before you make a decision. You may want to write down what you are going to be doing at home on a kind of "gift certificate" for your family. Be sure to *do* what you have promised.

Prayer

I know the Father loves me,
For He tells me in the rising sun.
I know the Father cares for me,
For I see it in the eyes of a certain someone.
Let the earth ring.
Let the people sing.
God is in love with His people.
God is in love with me.

(Gary Ault)

3

Belonging
to the Church

In This Chapter

You will review how it feels to be left out.

You will discover your identity as a member of the Catholic Church.

You will learn four attitudes you need to show your membership in God's Family.

Feeling Left Out

Jess is new at the school. On his first day, he is trying to be very polite. So, at the bus stop after classes, he stands back and waits for the older students to get on the bus. When it is his turn, there is no more room. The driver tells Jess that he will have to wait for the next bus. The other students laugh at Jess's mistake. Jess feels left out.

Carolyn knows she cannot afford to buy the same kinds of clothes the other girls are wearing. Her parents will not let her wear makeup or go out on dates yet. There is a group of girls Carolyn would really like to join. But she feels that she is not good enough to be part of the group. Carolyn feels left out.

Tryouts for the school basketball team were last week. Sergio and his three friends had spent hours working out together. They practiced for months. The day before the tryouts, Sergio broke his leg. His friends made the team. Sergio feels very left out.

Devon's friends are all talking about the Fathers' and Daughters' Breakfast. Devon really wants to go, but her parents are divorced, and her father lives two thousand miles away. Devon knows that she cannot go to the banquet alone. She feels very left out.

Andrew is short—almost a foot shorter than the more popular boys in the class. Girls either treat him like a little brother, or they make fun of his size. Andrew is never invited to mixed parties. He feels left out.

Questions

1. Give an example of a time when you felt left out of some event or group. How did this make you feel about yourself?
2. What are two or three things you do for fear of being left out?
3. Have you ever made someone else feel left out? Why?

Activities

1. In small groups, list as many reasons as you can (at least five) why a person might feel left out. Then, discuss (a) how a group can avoid making others feel left out and (b) how a person can deal with feelings of being left out.
2. Search the daily newspaper or watch the television news for stories of people who are left out. Report on one such situation. Your report should include (a) who is the in-group and who is being left out, (b) what is the reason the person is left out, and (c) what changes could be made in the situation to help the person who is feeling left out.

I Call You Friends

If someone asks you at a party, "Who are you?" it is not very likely you will answer, "I am Georgia Kubrick, and I did not get chosen for the debating team," or "I am Randy Copperman, and I *do not* belong to the Explorer Scouts, the YMCA, or the city soccer league."

You often identify yourself with the groups to which you belong. The reason for this is simple. Belonging is a very important part of personal identity. Part of your identity is your membership in the Catholic Church. You are a follower of Jesus Christ. You are someone who belongs to the group Jesus started.

Jesus lived in a society that had many kinds of outcasts. Shepherds were outcasts because they looked dirty and smelled bad, and because they did not read the *Torah* in the synagogue. The magi were outcasts because they did not follow the Law of Moses. The *Pharisees* were considered outcasts by the *Sadducees*, and the Sadducees were considered outcasts by the Pharisees.

Anyone who had a reputation as a sinner was an outcast from polite Jewish society. Lepers were feared. Samaritans were hated. Tax collectors, prostitutes, publicans, and even women were often left out of Jewish life.

Jesus knew that in His Father's kingdom there were no in-groups and no outcasts. All anyone who wished to belong had to do was have faith in Jesus and have a good heart. To be even more dramatic, Jesus chose as His friends, lepers, fishermen, tax collectors, prostitutes, Pharisees, Sadducees, women, sinners, and many more who were supposed to feel left out. His followers were those who knew they were loved by God and who wanted to love God in return.

Torah The first five books of the Hebrew Scripture—Genesis, Exodus, Leviticus, Numbers, and Deuteronomy. The Torah is also known as the Books of the Law or the Pentateuch.

Pharisee A class of Jewish leaders. They were the wise teachers of the Law of Moses. During the time of Jesus, some Pharisees taught that obedience to the Law was more important than anything. Jesus reminded the Pharisees that love was the most important law.

Sadducees A class of Jewish leaders. They were well educated and very traditional in religious matters. They did not accept any part of Jewish teaching that was not written in the Torah.

"There are many rooms in My Father's kingdom," Jesus once said. "I am indeed going to prepare a place for you, and then I shall come back to take you with Me" *(John 14:2)*. Jesus was saying that there is room for everyone in God's group because everyone is worthwhile and valuable. By your baptism, you have become a member of the Christian Church. Because you were baptized into the Roman Catholic Church, you belong in the Catholic Christian Family.

Many members of groups wear uniforms, special hats, pins, or badges to show that they have not been left out. They proudly display that they are members of a club or organization. The badge of your belonging to the Church (like the cross) has four arms. On each of the arms could be written a word: one, catholic, apostolic, holy. These words describe the four marks, or signs, of the Church. These signs show on the outside what is going on inside a Christian's heart.

1. *One.* People who belong to the Church try to put aside their own differences and become one in Christ Jesus.
2. *Catholic.* People who belong to the Church want to leave no one out. They reach out to everyone in the world.
3. *Apostolic.* People who belong to the Church want to be faithful to the teachings of Jesus and the Apostles. They follow and obey those teachings.
4. *Holy.* People who belong to the Church know that the greatest enemy is selfishness. They work hard to show by the way they live that Jesus has meaning for everyone in the world today.

Struggle to Be One

It was getting very late, but the pope could not sleep. On the next morning, his dream was going to come true. Pope John XXIII paced back and forth in his private chapel. The eighty-year-old man fingered his rosary. Between Hail Marys, his mind jumped ahead to the morning—October 11, 1962, the feast of the Motherhood of Mary, and the first day of the Vatican *Council* II. Pope John knew that the people of the world were sick with worry and sin and fear. He knew that the world needed a good dose of the medicine of mercy. He prayed that what the bishops were meeting to accomplish would dispense some of that medicine.

The old pope sat down for a moment and stared at the tabernacle. As he prayed, he remembered Jesus talking with His disciples at the Last Supper. "Father," Jesus said, "I pray for those who will believe in Me, that all may be one as You, Father, are in Me, and I am in You. I pray that they may be one in us, that the world may believe that You sent Me *(John 17:20–21).*

There were tears in the old pope's eyes—tears of hope and excitement. With all his heart, he prayed, using the simple, peasant Italian of his youth. "Papa," he prayed, "I do not pray for me, Your Angelo. I do not even pray for all my brother bishops from all over the world. Tonight, I look at all the beautiful people who want so badly to love You and to be happy. Papa, may what we do here help answer the prayer of Your Son—that all may be one."

Council A meeting of the pope and bishops to discuss Church teaching. From 1962 to 1964, the last council of the Church was held in Rome. It was called Vatican Council II.

Open to All

Mother Drexel sat before the Blessed Sacrament in her wheelchair. For the past forty years, Mother Mary Katherine Drexel (Kate as her family called her) had led a group of strong and dedicated women in a very special mission. She and her sisters had worked so that native Americans and blacks received the welcome and the assistance of the Catholic Church.

Mother Mary Katherine knew that the very word *catholic* meant "for everyone." She would never rest until she had done everything in her power to make the Church open for minority groups in the United States. She had come from a very wealthy Philadelphia family. But for Kate, wealth meant nothing if it were not used to help others. But Kate had given

more to help others than just her money. She gave herself. She founded the Sisters of the Blessed Sacrament for one purpose—to help blacks and native Americans. She traveled back and forth across the country, founding schools, visiting her sisters, and revitalizing the missions.

Mother Mary Katherine had been hit with a stroke. She could no longer travel and visit her sisters. But she could still pray for the work of the religious order she had started. Every day she wrote letters to her sisters. Her prayers and her letters had the same theme. "God our Father will help us be open to everyone. He will help us tell the blacks and the Indians that in His house there is room for everybody. We are not alone in our work. God is with us, and He is all we need."

Faithful to Death

The two women huddled together in the corner of the hut. Quietly they talked about the teaching of the Apostles, the great love of Jesus, and the need to be faithful to God. The women were so joyful in the discussion it was hard to believe that they were waiting to be murdered.

Vibia Perpetua and her friend and servant, Felicitas, had been arrested by the soldiers of the Roman Empire in the city of Carthage, North Africa, in A.D. 202. Perpetua was twenty-two years old, and Felicitas was about eighteen.

Emperor Caesar Severus had demanded that all the Christians in North Africa be rounded up and forced to give up their faithfulness to Jesus. He ordered them to offer worship to Serapis, the Egyptian god of the dead who was a favorite of the emperor. And now six young Christians were together in this hut waiting for death. Over and over again, they had refused to be disloyal to Jesus and the teachings of His Apostles. Again and again, they had refused to worship Serapis.

Now, their time had come. Perpetua and Felicitas were taken from the hut into the arena. They were

tied up in nets and were attacked by wild cows. The animals struck the nets again and again. After a while, both the animals and the crowds became bored. So, a gladiator was sent out to kill Perpetua and Felicitas with a sword.

Badly wounded, the two strong women walked to the place of death. They gave each other the kiss of peace. Perpetua called out to her brother who was also waiting for death. "You must all stand fast in the faith and love one another," she said, "and do not be weakened by what we have gone through." With that, the gladiator's sword sent Perpetua and Felicitas to be with Jesus forever.

Being Holy

The radio reporter leaned toward the energetic old man sitting before him. The reporter was a little afraid. The churchman was so calm, so strong. "What is death for you, Your Eminence?" the reporter asked.

Joseph Cardinal Cardijn smiled and answered, "It is to carry on living; it is a passover, a transition."

"And what will you be doing in heaven?" the reporter continued.

"The same thing I am doing now. I will work for youth."

All his life, Joseph Cardijn had a passion. He wanted the Gospel of Jesus Christ to be real for people, not only in church at Sunday Mass. He wanted the Gospel of Jesus to reach into factories, markets, office buildings, and farms. Joseph was sure that holiness meant following Jesus in the simple actions of everyday life.

Joseph was sure that Christ had at His disposal a whole army who could help make this happen— young people. The Belgian priest organized the young people of Europe, North America, Latin America, Asia, and Africa into groups dedicated to following Jesus and helping people live full and dignified lives. Joseph Cardijn's groups were called the Young Christian Workers.

Joseph always identified with the poor around the world—black miners in South Africa, Indian banana workers in Nicaragua, street kids in New York, factory workers in France. His young people met in basements, lobbies, garages, parish halls, or any place they could squeeze together. Their meetings were to help them bring the Gospel into their own lives and into the lives of others. At each meeting, they would use the same procedure—observe, judge, act. The young people would look at a problem in their lives. Then, they would study a Christian principle or Gospel teaching that would help the problem. Finally, they would decide on an action to help solve the problem. These meetings helped the young people follow Jesus where they lived and worked.

In 1963, Pope Paul VI made Joseph a cardinal. He was embarrassed. He complained to the pope that he had spent all his life with the working class. How could he become a cardinal? The pope told him that he would still speak for the working class but with more influence.

Joseph Cardijn died in 1967. Before his death, he repeated over and over, "We are at the beginning—always at the beginning. All my life, God has been so good to me!"

Come to the Banquet

You are a part of the same Family that supported and cared for these great people. Jesus is inviting you today to be an active part of the Church, just as He was inviting the people of His own time.

A man was giving a large dinner and he invited many. At dinner time he sent his servant to say to those invited, "Come along, everything is ready now." But they began to excuse themselves, one and all.... Then the man said to his servant, "Go out quickly into the streets and alleys of the town and bring in the poor and the crippled, the blind and the lame." The servant reported, after some time, "Your orders have been carried out, my lord, and there is still room." The master then said to the servant, "Go out into the highways and along the hedgerows and force them to come in. I want my house to be full."

(Luke 14:16–23)

You will always face enemies as part of your membership in the Church—your following of Jesus. The enemy of unity is intolerance. The enemy of catholicity is prejudice. The enemy of apostolicity is disloyalty. The enemy of holiness is selfishness.

But as long as you are growing in those four signs, and as long as you are fighting those enemies in yourself and in others, you are wearing your badge. You are showing that you are proud and happy to be a friend and follower of Jesus.

Questions

1. Why did Jesus spend time with people who were considered outcasts?
2. What are the four signs that could be found on a Christian membership badge? Briefly explain each.
3. How did each of the special people in this chapter (Pope John, Kate Drexel, Perpetua and Felicitas, and Cardinal Cardijn) show his or her belonging to the Church?
4. What is the enemy of each of the four marks of the Church?
5. Pick one of the four signs of the Church. What is one way you show that sign in the way you act?

Activities

1. Form small groups and read one of the Gospel stories listed below. Consider how Jesus treated the person who was left out. Then discuss how you can apply the example of Jesus to your own actions and relationships.
   a. The centurion's servant (Matthew 8:5–13)
   b. The call of Matthew (Matthew 9:9–13)
   c. The Canaanite woman (Matthew 15:21–28)
   d. The penitent woman (Luke 7:36–50)
   e. The Good Samaritan (Luke 10:25–37)
   f. The ten lepers (Luke 17:11–19)
   g. The Samaritan woman (John 4:1–30)
2. Write a résumé to God, listing all the reasons why you should be included in His kingdom.

Leave No One Out

Use the chart as a guide to plan how you can share your sense of belonging to the Church with others. Work in small groups. First, choose some situation in which people are being treated like outcasts. Secondly, choose one of the signs of the Church (one, holy, catholic, apostolic) which can help solve the problem. Discuss how this sign will help. Then, plan a strategy for changing the situation. You will be using Cardinal Cardijn's famous observe, judge, act. *Note:* Try to choose one situation for each of the marks of the Church.

Problem/Observe	Sign/Judge	Strategy/Act
	One	
	Holy	
	Catholic	
	Apostolic	

Review

Read the following sentences. Each one is a situation which needs one of the four marks of the Church. Label each sentence with the correct one (*U* for unity, *H* for holiness, *C* for catholic, and *A* for apostolic).

1. ____ Jill feels that she is better than the Protestant young people because she follows the pope and they do not.

2. ____ A group of boys are planning to break the windows in Mr. Fritch's market.

3. ＿＿ Jody thinks that she can choose to believe whatever she wants to. What she learns in class is just not important.

4. ＿＿ Jack doesn't think it's fair that the youth club from the central city are allowed to use Saint Cyril's gym for practice.

5. ＿＿ Cody tells everyone that the Church's teaching about going to Sunday Mass is silly.

6. ＿＿ Barbara has the opinion that Saint Martha's should repair the youth room in the parish hall before sending money to the African missionaries.

7. ＿＿ Bill uses bad language around some of his friends so that they won't think he is too religious.

Projects

1. Make a badge or other sign of your belonging to the Church. Include on the badge symbols of each of the four marks of the Church. Explain the badge to your family at home.

2. As an ongoing project, make a "Belonging to the Church" scrapbook. Collect articles and pictures which illustrate each of the four marks of the Church. You may want to work in committees for this exercise.

Prayer

We will walk with each other.
We will walk hand in hand . . .
And together we'll spread the news
That God is in our land.
And they'll know we are Christians by our love,
   by our love.
Yes, they'll know we are Christians by our love.

(Rev. Peter Scholtes)

4

Forgiven

In This Chapter

You will recall how feelings of failure can make you think less of yourself.

You will learn that your identity as a Christian includes God's loving forgiveness.

You will learn that you can show your Christian identity by being a forgiving person.

Feeling like a Failure

t hurts not to be liked. It hurts even more when you somehow made someone not like you or get really angry at you. Maybe you once had an experience like Sharon's. She didn't study for the test. She got some very easy answers wrong. The teacher said to her after class, "Sharon, how could you be so careless? Your test paper was one of the worst I have ever seen. One more like this and I am going to have a talk with your parents."

To make matters worse, somebody overheard the teacher. On the way home, Sharon heard a chant behind her, "Shaaaron, how *could* you be *so* careless? Your test was the worst!" Then, laughter. She felt humiliated, hurt, and even a little worthless. If someone asked her at that moment who she was, Sharon might have snapped back in reply, "I am the idiot who didn't study for the test." She would feel like a failure, and she would probably feel that the world was full of enemies.

Read the following statements. After each statement, ask yourself three questions: (1) What do you think happened? (2) What is the person feeling? and (3) What would help the person get a better picture of him or herself?

1. "I can't do anything right! Every time I try something new, I make a mess of it."
2. "I was afraid I was going to be punished, so I lied. But I got caught in my lie. No one will ever trust me again."
3. "I was so jealous that I threw her test paper in the trash. Somebody saw me do it and reported me to the teacher. Now what is going to happen?"
4. "When I broke the window, my father yelled at me. He was very angry. He must think I am really careless."
5. "I called him all kinds of names. He used to be my best friend, but now he'll never speak to me again."
6. "She has a real grudge against me. No matter what I do, she thinks I am no good."

Questions

1. How do you feel when you fail at something or do something wrong?
2. How do you react when adults criticize you?
3. How do you react when your friends criticize you?

Activity

Make a list of words which can tear people down and another list of words which can help build people up. Then, choose one or two words from each list and describe how you would feel if those words were used to describe you.

Come Back to Me

No matter how you feel about yourself, no matter what goes wrong, no matter what you do wrong, or what anyone says to you, one thing remains true: God still thinks you are great and still loves you. God has left traces of His forgiving love throughout the history of His People. These acts of forgiveness are like God's footsteps in the world.

When the first people sinned, God forgave them and loved them. He did not leave them. When the people wandering in the desert forgot about God and grumbled against Him, He forgave them and led them into the *Land of Promise.*

In the Hebrew Scriptures, there is the story of Hosea the Prophet. People used to tell the story of Hosea to remind one another just how loving and forgiving God is. Hosea was married to a woman who was a failure in everybody's eyes. Gomer, his wife, was a wicked woman. She kept running away from Hosea. But every time she ran away, Hosea went after her and urged her to come back. Hosea really loved Gomer, and nothing she could do would ever change that.

The story of Hosea and his wife, Gomer, has a very simple lesson: Nothing you do can change the simple truth of God's love. Jesus came to tell people more about God's love and forgiveness. He wanted them to see that being forgiven by God was part of their identity as His followers. In all the teaching Jesus did, He had a simple fourfold message about God's forgiveness and love for each person.

1. No matter what, come back home to God.
2. No matter what, try to see the good in yourself that God your Father sees in you.
3. No matter what, accept as a gift the care, love, and concern of God your Father.
4. No matter what, be willing to forgive others.

Land of Promise Israel, the place that God promised to His People when He led them out of Egypt.

The Homecoming

If you have ever been separated from your family, you know the happiness of coming home. You know just what Jesus meant when He told this story about coming home to God the Father.

"A man had two sons. The younger of them said to his father, 'Father, give me a share of the estate that is coming to me.' So the father divided up the property. Some days later this younger son collected all his belongings and went off to a distant land, where he squandered his money on dissolute living. After he had spent everything, a great famine broke out in that country and he was in dire need. So he attached himself to one of the propertied class of the place, who sent him to his farm to take care of the pigs. He longed to fill his belly with the husks that were fodder for the pigs, but no one made a move to give him anything. Coming to his senses at last, he said: 'How many hired hands at my father's place have more than enough to eat, while here I am starving! I will break away and return to my father, and say to him, Father, I have sinned against God and against you; I no longer deserve to be called your son. Treat me like one of your hired hands.' With that he set off for his father's house. While he was still a long way off, his father caught sight of him and was deeply moved. He ran out to meet him, threw his arms around his neck, and kissed him."

(Luke 15:11–20)

The Penitent

When you have failed at something, when you have done wrong, or when other people think badly of you, it is very hard for you to see the good there is in you. Jesus had that in mind when He gave another of His forgiveness lessons.

There was a certain Pharisee who invited Jesus to dine with him. Jesus went to the Pharisee's home

and reclined to eat. A woman known in the town to be a sinner learned that He was dining in the Pharisee's home. She brought in a vase of perfumed oil and stood behind Him at His feet, weeping so that her tears fell upon His feet. Then she wiped them with her hair, kissing them and perfuming them with oil. When His host, the Pharisee, saw this, he said to himself, "If this man were a prophet, He would know who and what sort of woman this is that touches Him—that she is a sinner." . . . Jesus said to him: "You see this woman? I came to your home and you provided Me with no water for My feet. She has washed My feet with her tears and wiped them with her hair. . . . I tell you, that is why her many sins are forgiven— because of her great love."

(Luke 7:36–47)

The Crippled Man

When you are feeling like a failure, it is very difficult for you—or anyone—to accept someone else's care and concern. It is hard to believe that somebody could reach out to you when you are so down on yourself. Jesus knew that fact, but He wanted people to know that their powerful and loving Father would always reach out to them.

> One day Jesus was teaching, and the power of the Lord made Him heal. . . . Some men came along carrying a crippled man on a mat. They were trying to bring him in and lay him before Jesus; but they found no way of getting him through because of the crowd, so they went up on the roof. There they let him down with his mat through the tiles into the middle of the crowd before Jesus. Seeing their faith, Jesus said, "My friend, your sins are forgiven you. . . . To make it clear to you that the Son of Man has authority on earth to forgive sins, . . . I say to you, get up! Take your mat with you, and return to your house." At once the man stood erect before them. He picked up the mat he had been lying on and went home praising God.
>
> *(Luke 5:17–25)*

Act Forgiven

Knowing that there is nothing you can do to make God stop loving you is another answer to that question, "Who am I?" The answer is "I am forgiven by God." The best way to show that part of your Christian identity is to act forgiven. And Jesus taught just how to do that by telling a very harsh story about a man who did not act forgiven.

> "The reign of God may be said to be like a king who decided to settle accounts with his officials. When he began his auditing, one was brought in who owed him a huge amount. As he had no way of paying it, his master ordered him to be sold, along with his wife, his children, and all his property, in payment of the debt. At that the official prostrated himself in *homage* and said, 'My lord, be patient with me and I will pay you back in full.' Moved with pity, the master let the official go and wrote off the debt.

Homage An act by which a person shows that he or she is willing to obey God's laws. Catholics pay homage to God at Mass.

"But when that same official went out, he met a fellow servant who owed him a mere fraction of what he himself owed. He seized him and throttled him. 'Pay back what you owe,' he demanded. His fellow servant dropped to his knees and began to plead with him, 'Just give me time and I will pay you back in full.' But he would hear none of it. Instead, he had him put in jail until he paid back what he owed.

"When his fellow servants saw what had happened, they were badly shaken and went to their master to report the whole incident. His master sent for him and said, 'You worthless wretch! I canceled your entire debt when you pleaded with me. Should you not have dealt mercifully with your fellow servant, as I dealt with you?' Then, in anger, the master handed him over to the torturers until he paid back all that he owed."

(Matthew 18:23–35)

Jesus finished the story with a warning: "My heavenly Father will treat you that way if you do not forgive one another in your heart." As a follower of Jesus, being forgiven is part of what you are. So, if you come home, if you see God's goodness in yourself, if you accept God's care and concern, and if you forgive others, you are showing just how proud and happy you are to be a follower of Jesus Christ.

Questions

1. Why is forgiveness such an important part of love?
2. What are the four ways you can experience the forgiving love of God your Father? Give an example of each.
3. How do you react when someone forgives you for something?
4. How do you show others that you forgive them?

Activities

1. In small groups, choose and read one of the forgiveness stories listed below. Then, discuss how the people in the stories might have felt about the forgiveness that was given by Jesus.
   a. Luke 23:39–43 — the Good Thief
   b. John 21:15–19 — Saint Peter
   c. Luke 23:33–34 — the Roman soldiers
2. Find a news story which shows the need for forgiveness. Write a brief description of how a Christian (part of whose identity is forgiveness) would handle the situation.

Forgiven and Forgiving

The activity below will help you see that forgiveness is a very important part of your following Jesus. When you have completed the questions, discuss in small groups or in class how you can remind one another that no matter what, you are loved by God.

1. Describe three times when you have felt the need for forgiveness.

   a. _____

   b. _____

   c. _____

2. Describe three times when someone needed your forgiveness.

   a. _____

   b. _____

   c. _____

3. How do you feel when you have done something wrong?

   _____

4. How do you feel when somebody has hurt you?

   _____

5. In your own words, what does it mean to you that God your Father is a forgiving God?

   _____

6. List three practical ways you can act forgiven.

   a. _____

   b. _____

   c. _____

Review

Take each step in the fourfold message Jesus gave about forgiveness and briefly describe what it means. Then, give one example of how you can put that message to use.

Message	Meaning	Use
Come Home		
See Goodness		
Accept Concern		
Forgive Others		

Projects

1. Plan a reconciliation service around the theme of "No matter what, God forgives His children." Pages 284–285 of your Handbook will help you. The songs, prayers, and readings you select should show how God's love lasts forever.

2. Hold small-group discussions on the relationship between forgiveness and punishment. Can a person be forgiven and still receive punishment for something that has been done? How can punishment help you hear the fourfold message of forgiveness? Share the results of your discussion with your family.

Prayer

All-holy Father,
You have shown us Your mercy
and made us a new creation
in the likeness of Your Son.
Make us living signs of Your love
for the whole world to see.
We ask this through Christ our Lord.

(From the Rite of Penance)

5

Gifted
by the Spirit

In This Chapter

*You will see how the Holy
Spirit helps you become your
best self.*

*You will study some of the gifts
the Holy Spirit gives to you.*

*You will learn how you can
share these gifts with others.*

Rosary Hill

other Alphonsa was dead. On her nightstand was a notebook open to a page of jottings. "If there are any flowers of selfishness left in the garden of our lives," the jottings read, "let us gather them as a gift for Jesus Christ.... I will obey God anywhere, anytime, with courage!... I will see all things only through the presence of God.... I will regard creatures in the spirit of Jesus Christ."

Mother Alphonsa was born Rose Hawthorne in 1851. She was the daughter of the famous American author Nathaniel Hawthorne. She grew up in the wealthy literary society of New York and New England. When she was very young, Rose traveled around the world with her parents. When she was nineteen years old, she married another American writer named George Lathrop. Their only child, Francis, died as a baby.

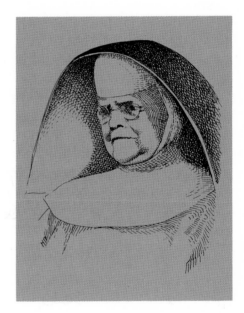

After the death of their son, Rose and George moved to New York. There, Rose became friends with Emma Lazarus, the person who wrote the saying, "Give me your tired and your poor," which is inscribed on the Statue of Liberty. Emma contracted what was then and is now one of the most frightening of diseases—cancer. The suffering of her good friend deeply affected Rose.

George Lathrop continued his writing, but he began to develop a serious drinking problem. And so, he and Rose were having a great deal of trouble. They moved from place to place. They were always trying to make new starts because they really wanted to save their marriage.

In New London, Connecticut, they began attending a Catholic church with friends. They were both received as members of the Catholic Church on March 19, 1891—the feast of Saint Joseph. Both were very happy to be identified with these followers of

Jesus. They loved to go to Mass and receive the sacraments. Rose began going to Mass every day. Rose also began to spend time working with the poor and suffering. She remembered that her friend, Emma, died among friends and with the best of care, but poor victims of cancer died in poverty and horrible pain.

During this time, George and Rose separated as husband and wife. Their life together had become unbearable. Rose received permission from the Church to leave her husband. With her home life shattered, Rose moved back to New York. She knew she had to make some changes in her way of life. She really wanted to learn from her mistakes. She wanted to spend the rest of her life helping others. In particular, she wanted to help the poor victims of incurable cancer. For these poor suffering people, the only choice was to die on Blackwell's Island—New York City's last stopping point for the dying poor. Blackwell's Island was a terrible place without hope or dignity.

Rose's life became a flurry of activity supported by great reverence and prayer. With a friend, Alice Huber, she became a member of the Dominican *Third Order*. Soon, they received permission to start their own community and to wear the Dominican *habit*. Their new group was called the Daughters of Saint Dominic.

They opened a house for cancer victims in New York City that was too small the day it opened. They prayed for a new and larger place. In 1901, they received the chance to buy a vacant monastery in Hawthorne, New York. Rose (now called Mother Alphonsa) called the place Rosary Hill. Her incurable cancer patients had a beautiful setting in which to spend the last days of their lives.

Almost every week, young women came to Mother Alphonsa at Rosary Hill. They sought her advice. They wanted to join her. They wanted to learn from her how to grow in their Catholic faith and in their active working for others. Mother Alphonsa knew

Third order A special way for lay people to be a part of the work and spirit of a religious order without becoming sisters or brothers. Members of third orders say special prayers and follow certain rules. The Franciscans, Dominicans, Carmelites, and others have third orders.

Habit The special clothing worn by members of religious orders. Dominicans wear a white habit with a black cape.

what it meant to be a follower of Jesus. She knew that nobody can live their whole life at once. Living to Mother Alphonsa meant growing and changing every day, and having the wisdom to learn from her mistakes. It meant having reverence for God and for her fellow human beings. It meant having the courage to change, to help others, to take risks, as well as to seek and give help.

As the jottings on Mother Alphonsa's nightstand showed, she was growing in her Christian identity right up to the day she died.

Questions

1. What were some of the changes Rose Hawthorne had to make in her life?
2. What were some of the meanings life had for Rose?
3. Describe a change you had to make in your life. How did you discover the need to change? How did you make the change?

Activities

1. In small groups, choose one of the people listed below. Read the two Scripture passages. Then, discuss the changes and growth that took place in the people.
   a. Paul—Acts 8:1–3, Acts 12:13–43
   b. Peter— Mark 8:31–33, Acts 2:14–36
   c. James and John— Mark 10:35–45, Acts 4:5–23
   d. Nicodemus— John 3:1–21, John 19:38–42
2. Write a short play or story, or draw a picture of what the world would be like if there were *no* changes and *no* growth.

Growth in the Spirit

You have a lot in common with Rose Hawthorne Lathrop. First of all, you are a member of the same Christian family—the Catholic Church. The Mass you celebrate and the sacraments you receive are the same Mass and sacraments that gave so much joy to Mother Alphonsa. There is something else you have in common. Jesus has given you the same gifts to help you grow that Rose received. When you were baptized and when you receive the sacrament of Confirmation, Jesus is keeping a special promise to you.

The Promise

Jesus watched His friends eating. He knew that they were going to have a most difficult time being His followers. He had taught them so many lessons in so short a time. Jesus looked ahead at all the choices His followers had to make, changes they would experience, risks they would be taking, and the help they would need.

Even though there was sadness in His heart at this last meal with His friends, Jesus smiled with love. He cleared His throat to get their attention, and He made the Apostles a promise.

"I will ask the Father and
He will give you another *Paraclete*—
to be with you always:
the Spirit of truth,
whom the world cannot accept,
since it neither sees Him nor
  recognizes Him;
but you can recognize Him
because He remains with you. . . .
Much I have told you while I
  was still with you;

Paraclete A title for the Holy Spirit. The word *paraclete* means "special helper."

the Paraclete, the Holy Spirit
whom the Father will send in My name,
will instruct you in everything,
and remind you of all that I told you."

(John 14:16–17, 25–26)

The Apostles received the promised Spirit on Pentecost. The Holy Spirit helped the Apostles in many ways. The ways He used are often called the gifts of the Holy Spirit.

The Holy Spirit—the promise of Jesus—is given to each new member of the Church in the sacraments of Baptism and Confirmation. You have received the Spirit, and you are always receiving His gifts. Just as you need food, sleep, exercise, shelter, and clothing to care for your physical growth and maturity, you also need help to grow as a person—a follower of Jesus.

Wisdom

Thousands and thousands of choices go into your growing up. You learn how to love others. You learn how to recognize the truth when you see it. You learn from your mistakes so that you can make changes in the way you think and act.

Your Jewish ancestors knew the need for all this. They recognized this quality in people, and they called the quality wisdom. They sought out wise people. They wrote down the teachings of these people in a special section of the Scripture called the *Wisdom literature*. Wisdom is one of the gifts of the Spirit. But like all gifts, wisdom is a gift that you use as you need it—you gradually learn how to choose, to decide, to act, to love, and to change.

If you watch a child learning how to tie his or her shoes, you can learn a lesson about wisdom. When you tie your shoes, you think nothing of it. You do it almost automatically. But a little child has to concentrate. The stubby fingers go so slowly. Often it takes ten or more minutes for the child to finish the task. Even then, the knots are loose and sloppy. But

Wisdom literature The books of the Bible which give advice on how to live. The seven wisdom books are Job, Psalms, Proverbs, Ecclesiastes, Song of Songs, Wisdom, and Sirach.

there is a great sense of satisfaction on the face of the child.

The gift of wisdom grows with you. Decisions and choices you make today only with difficulty will become almost automatic later on. If you use the gift of wisdom, you will grow in wisdom. You will become a mature member of the Church. But you cannot grow alone. There is another gift of the Holy Spirit for that.

Counsel

As you grow and mature, you realize that you cannot solve every problem by yourself—you need help. Children know they are helpless. They depend on older people for everything. But as they grow and become more independent, it becomes harder to decide when help is needed and when it is not. Jesus recognized that need, too. He knew that if His followers were going to grow, they were going to have

to know when to seek help and when to give it. They needed to learn how to listen to advice and how to give it to others. So, the Spirit gives the gift of counsel, or right judgment.

Right now, you are still very dependent on others for the things you need, the skills you have to develop, and the choices you have to make. The more you grow and mature—the more you use the gift of counsel—the easier it will be for you to know how to decide when to give and receive help from others.

The Holy Spirit keeps the followers of Jesus alive and growing. The gift of counsel helps you be an active part of the group by sharing what you know and do with others. You also receive help, encouragement, challenge, and even correction from other followers of Jesus. So, part of your Christian identity is the way you give and receive help.

Courage

Rose Hawthorne learned quickly that life is not always easy. You have that in common with her, too. Some of the choices you have to make are really hard. If you want to be recognized as a follower of Jesus, you will not always be able to do everything everybody else is doing. It is very frightening for a person your age to be different, to say no, to always do what you know is right. But Rose and you both received the gift of courage from the Holy Spirit.

From the earliest days of the Church, Christians were seen as people of great courage—people who took risks to follow Jesus. Remember, it was illegal in the Roman Empire for a person to follow Jesus. The early Christians faced prison and even death. Yet, the Holy Spirit helped the early Christians lean on one another for strength. Their love for Jesus and for one another was stronger than the bars of a jail or the swords of the gladiators.

Down through the centuries, the followers of Jesus have taken great chances to feed the hungry or to give the thirsty something to drink. They have traveled all over the world to share the good news of Jesus. Even today the followers of Jesus take great risks in Poland, Russia, China, and other places to share their faith and live what Jesus taught in the Gospel.

The risks you take right now may not seem so great. You do not work with the incurably sick or travel to faraway places. It is not illegal for you to follow Jesus. But every time you decide to act like a member of the Church, you are using the gift of courage. When you choose to do what is right and help others do what is right—even when it is hard— you are acting courageously.

Reverence

The inspiration you need to keep strong your sense of belonging to the People of God comes from another gift of the Holy Spirit—reverence, or *piety*. Rose Hawthorne had a great respect for God and for all of God's creation. That respect translated itself into prayer and action. You are using the Holy Spirit's gift of reverence when you pray and when you treat creation with respect.

Piety A gift of the Holy Spirit which helps people worship God. Praying is sometimes called an act of piety.

A reverent person knows how important it is to spend time with God. A reverent person knows how to act with courtesy in church, in school, at home, and with friends. A reverent person looks at all of God's gifts with gratitude and concern.

When you take time to be with God and to talk to Him, you are growing in reverence. When you treat adults with respect, you are growing in reverence. When you show concern for the needs of others, you are showing this special gift of the Holy Spirit.

Other Gifts

There are other traditional gifts of the Spirit, too. The gift of knowledge helps you learn about your faith. The gift of understanding helps you put what you know into action. The gift of wonder, or awe, helps you see how important God is and helps you recognize signs of His love.

Whenever you use these gifts of the Holy Spirit, you feel the effects of the promise Jesus made at the Last Supper. You are growing and changing as a follower of Jesus. Like any gift, the gifts of the Holy Spirit can be shared with others. When you use and share these gifts, you are saying to the whole world, "I am a Christian. I am proud and happy to be recognized as a follower of Jesus!"

Questions

1. What was the promise Jesus made to His friends at the Last Supper?
2. What are the gifts of the Holy Spirit?
3. How have you used these gifts in the past? Give an example of each.

Activities

1. Choose one of the Scripture passages listed below. Briefly discuss how this passage reminds you of the gifts of the Holy Spirit. Then, choose one phrase from the passage and use it to make a bookmark or other personal reminder that you have been gifted by the Holy Spirit.
   a. 1 Corinthians 2:1–10
   b. 1 Corinthians 12:4–11
   c. 2 Thessalonians 2:15–17
2. Begin a roster of gifts of the Spirit. Find examples of each of the gifts as they are being used by the people in your family and parish. This could be an ongoing activity for home and for class.

A Plan of Growth

Nobody gets angry at an acorn for not being an oak tree. Nobody gets upset with a tadpole because it is not a frog. The same is true of you. Nobody is upset that you are not yet grown up. But there would be reason for concern if you refused to grow and to change. This section is a chance for you to plan your growth.

Go back over the first two sections of this chapter. Then, use the chart below as a guide to help you show and use the four gifts of the Holy Spirit that were discussed in the chapter. When you have finished, discuss what you have done. Then, the class should decide on one strategy to help one another use each of the gifts.

Plan	Wisdom	Counsel	Courage	Reverence
1. What does this gift mean to you?				
2. How do you use this gift now in your life?				
3. Give one example of how you plan to use this gift in the future.				
4. How will using this gift show you are a Christian?				

Review

Match the item in column B which best describes
each item in column A.

A	**B**
1. ___ Promise of Jesus	a. The ability to take risks to show you follow Jesus
2. ___ Wisdom	b. The ability to learn from mistakes
3. ___ Counsel	c. To send a special Person to help all to follow Him
4. ___ Reverence	d. The ability to seek and to give help
5. ___ Courage	e. The ability to respect God and creation

Projects

1. Write a prayer to the Holy Spirit asking Him to
   help you use His gifts.

2. Divide into seven groups, one for each of the
   situations listed below. Role play each situation
   for the class, with two endings: one which shows
   openness to the gift of the Spirit, and one which is
   not open to the gift of the Spirit.
   a. A needy person comes to your door and asks
      you for some money (Wisdom).
   b. You are tutoring a fifth grader who is not
      paying very much attention (Understanding).
   c. The two year old you are baby-sitting
      suddenly gets sick (Right judgment).
   d. A March of Dimes worker asks you to go door-
      to-door in your neighborhood to collect
      donations (Courage).
   e. A sick friend who missed school asks you to
      explain today's math lesson (Knowledge).
   f. You just got the last seat on the bus, by the
      door. An elderly man gets on (Reverence).
   g. You go camping at a nearby park (Wonder).

Prayer

Come, Holy Spirit,
Fill the hearts of your faithful.
Enkindle in them the fire of Your love.

(Traditional prayer to the Holy Spirit)

6

Born to
Live Forever

In This Chapter

You will recall how the death of Jesus looked like a victory for His enemies.

You will discover what the death and resurrection of Jesus means for you.

You will see how faith in everlasting life can help you grow.

A Visit to Calvary

sther and Simeon still staggered at the news. They pushed their way through the holiday crowds trying to get to the place called "the Skull" before it was too late.

Just a few hours earlier, they had been awakened by a frantic knocking at their door. It was John Mark with a terrible tale of Jesus being arrested and taken to the authorities. Then, bits of news came through the grapevine. Finally, the worst news of all—Jesus was being crucified as a traitor and a rebel.

Now, Esther and Simeon were trying to get to the place of crucifixion outside the city of Jerusalem. They wanted to see if they could help in any way. Simeon could hardly see for the tears pouring down his cheeks. "Not Jesus," he kept saying. "Not the Master!"

Memories shot through Esther's mind. Only last week, Jesus rode into the city like a hero. What had gone wrong? Just two days ago, she had heard Him speak. "The light is among you only a little while longer," He had said. "Walk while you still have it. While you have the light, keep faith in the light. Then, you will become children of light."

As the two reached the place called Calvary by the Romans, they heard the clanking of hammers against nails. They broke to the front of the crowd that was restrained by Pilate's own household guards. Esther screamed and Simeon went speechless. It was too late.

They would never forget the scene. In the quivering midday heat, the cross of Jesus stood etched against a yellow sky. His body was covered with sweat and blood. Someone with a twisted sense of humor had put a crown of thorns on His head. At the foot of the cross, the soldiers were playing games. Though the crowd was held back, Mary, the Mother

of Jesus, and His disciple John were standing nearby—praying and crying. A sign on the cross read, "Jesus of Nazareth, King of the Jews." It was an ugly sight.

"Where are the others?" Simeon thought. "What has happened? We put so much hope in Jesus. Is He just another failure? Why have His own friends rejected Him? Look how much suffering He is going through! He is dying. He said He is God's Son, and He is dying!"

Esther and Simeon stayed to pray and to hope. After a few hours, the crowd had grown quiet—even a bit embarrassed to be watching this execution. In the silence, they heard Jesus say, "Father, into Your hands I give My spirit." A little later, Jesus called out, "I am thirsty." One of the soldiers dipped a sponge in some wine, put the sponge on a stick, and put it to the lips of Jesus. After Jesus sipped the wine, He said, "It is finished." Then, He bowed His head and died.

Suddenly, Esther felt cold and lonely. Simeon thought that he had never seen such a dark and still afternoon.

Questions

1. On Calvary, Jesus met four of every person's worst enemies. What were they?
2. Why were so many of Jesus' friends missing from the scene at Calvary?
3. If you had been with Simeon and Esther, what would you have felt? What would you have said? What would you have done?

Activities

1. Re-create the story of the suffering and death of Jesus in a dramatic way. Use one of the New Testament stories of the crucifixion or tell the story in your own words.
   a. Matthew 26:47–27:51
   b. Mark 14:43–15:47
   c. Luke 22:47–23:56
   d. John 18:1–19:38
2. Pretend you are one of the early followers of Jesus. You have just heard about the death of Jesus. Write a short note to Mary, His Mother, telling how you have reacted to the news.

Life Forever

Failure and rejection, suffering and death are very, very frightening words. You are afraid of those four enemies, and so is everyone else. Nobody wants to be known as a failure. Nobody likes to be rejected or hated. Everyone tries to avoid suffering. And for most everyone, death is the worst enemy of all. On Calvary, Jesus got into a fight with all four of those enemies. And Jesus won—for you!

You see, Jesus was no stranger to these enemies. He was deeply troubled by the death of His friend Lazarus (John 11:33–35). He wept over the sins and

sufferings of Jerusalem (Luke 19:41). And He begged God to take away His own suffering and cross (Matthew 26:38–39). As a human being, Jesus Himself did not understand why good people suffer, why disasters strike, or why people have to die. But He continued to believe and to preach that failure, rejection, suffering, and death have some meaning. As He told His followers, "Blessed are those who mourn," and "Blessed are those who are persecuted" *(Matthew 5:4, 9)*. Jesus promised all those who believed in Him that no matter where they were, He would be there with them. Jesus promised to be with them not only in good times but also in times of suffering, discouragement, doubt, and despair.

Victory over Death

The crucifixion made Jesus *look* like a failure. Jesus did not *stay* a failure. He did not remain rejected. His sufferings ended. And Jesus beat death. "On the third day, He rose again."

With the resurrection, Jesus showed His friends that they would have life forever. All of a sudden, the words Jesus had said to His friend Martha made sense. "Whoever lives and believes in Me will never die" *(John 11:26).* The resurrection of Jesus was a great treasure handed down from believer to believer—right to you. The treasure is the fact that God your Father loves you so much that no failure, no rejection, no suffering—not even death—can keep you from Him. Saint Paul gave the treasure to the people of Rome with these words.

> I am certain that neither death nor life, neither angels nor principalities, neither the present nor the future, nor powers, neither height nor depth nor any other creature, will be able to separate us from the love of God that comes to us in Christ Jesus, our Lord.
>
> *(Romans 8:38–39)*

The *Orthodox* Christians have a song they sing at Eastertime which reminds them of the treasure. "Christ is risen from the dead. With death He has trampled death, and to those in the tombs He has given life." Instead of saying "hello" during Eastertime, these Christians greet one another with the words, "Christ is risen!" The answer is "He is truly risen."

Orthodox Eastern Christian Churches which have their own special worship and tradition but are separated from the pope. The word *orthodox* means "true believing."

God's Tramp

Benedict Joseph Labre was a mess! He was seen by all as a total failure. He was dirty. He had no home. Everyone thought he was crazy. He traveled throughout eighteenth century Europe visiting churches and shrines, and praying and begging for food. All he had ever wanted to be was a monk—to spend his life in a monastery working and praying. But every time he tried to join a monastery, he was turned away.

After many rejections, Benedict decided that the whole world would be his monastery. He made a rough, heavy wooden cross and began to travel. He wore a rosary around his neck. He spoke little, but when he did, he spoke about the love of God. He prayed constantly. Children threw stones at Benedict. People whispered behind his back. After many travels (which he called his *stations of the cross*), Benedict came to live and to beg in Rome.

The pilgrims to Rome came to notice that even though Benedict looked and smelled like the other beggars, he was different. They urged him to go to one of the homes for the poor. But Benedict continued to sleep on the streets, beg for crumbs, and speak about the love of God. During Holy Week, in 1783, Benedict collapsed on the steps of the Church of the Madonna dei Monte. The butcher, Zaccarelli, took the dying man to his home and put him into his own bed. Two days later, as the Good Friday liturgy was being sung in the churches, Benedict died—with a smile on his face.

The children of Rome—the same ones who had thrown stones at Benedict—ran through the street shouting, "The saint is dead." Today, the tramp who was a failure, who was rejected by everyone, who suffered hunger and pain, and who died in a stranger's bed, is called Saint Benedict Joseph Labre. He is alive with Jesus. He will never die.

Stations of the cross A traditional devotion which consists of meditating on the sufferings of Jesus. The fourteen stations of the cross are usually found on the side walls of Catholic churches.

Little Deaths

You do not live like Saint Labre. But you do know what it feels like to fail. You know how it hurts to be rejected. You have felt pain and maybe even sickness. All of these events are like little deaths. You can see them as part of learning to live forever. You can see them as part of what you are.

The wonderful part about being a follower of Jesus is that you can help one another remember that mistakes are not fatal. You can help one another remember that Jesus has already met the worst enemies, and He has defeated them.

Everyone is going to experience bodily death. There is no way to avoid that. So, it is important to be prepared for death. But death is not permanent. Jesus has provided the sign that resurrection from the dead is part of living. After you die, the good you have done will be celebrated. You will be judged on the way you have lived on earth. You will live forever.

The way you handle the little deaths of living will show how you can handle death itself. Part of your growing as a Catholic Christian is your ability to face failure, rejection, suffering, and even death with a good sense of your own value and worth. Part of that value is very exciting. You are someone so loved by God that you will someday rise from the dead—you will live forever!

Questions

1. How did Jesus show that He was aware of the four enemies of life?
2. What is the meaning of the resurrection of Jesus?
3. How did the life of Saint Benedict Labre show the resurrection of Jesus?
4. What are your feelings about failure? rejection? suffering? death?

Activities

1. In your Handbook, page 278, look up the celebration of Easter. How do the symbols of Easter remind you that you are a person who lives forever? Choose one of the symbols as your own personal reminder. Share it with your family.

2. In small groups, choose one of the Scripture passages listed below. Read the passage in the group. Then, discuss how you can help one another remember that you will live forever.
   a. John 11:23–27
   b. John 20:24–29
   c. Romans 6:1–10

Resurrection

he resurrection is not something that only occurs after you die. The resurrection happens every time you work through failure or rejection and reach some sort of comfort. The resurrection occurs every time you work through suffering and experience God's personal concern for you. The resurrection occurs whenever you can look back on a difficult time and see how the Holy Spirit was with you and working for your good.

To help you better understand the resurrection, answer the following sentences. Then, spend time comparing your answers with those of your classmates.

1. Give examples in your life of times when you have been discouraged by one of the following.

   a. Failure: _____

   b. Rejection: _____

   c. Suffering: _____

2. Describe what that discouragement felt like in each of the above situations.

   _____

3. List who or what seemed to help you feel better in each of the situations.

   _____

4. List practical ways you can help someone who is feeling discouraged in each of the situations.

   _____

5. How could your belief in God's love bring you from "death" to "resurrection" in each of the above situations?

   _____

Review

Copy the chart below. For each of the four enemies, describe how you and your fellow members of the Church can support one another in facing these enemies.

Enemy	Christian Attitude	Mutual Support
Failure		
Rejection		
Suffering		
Death		

Projects

1. Use one of the arts (poetry, short story, painting, drawing, or music) to portray the meaning of the resurrection of Jesus in the everyday lives of His followers. Share your creations in class.

2. Research various Christian funeral customs. List them and show how each reminds believers that they will live forever.

3. As a family project, plan an evening of watching television purposefully. Keep a scorecard on how the programs (and the commercials) treat failure, rejection, suffering, and death. Share your scorecard in class.

Prayer

Father,
Through the death and resurrection of Your Son,
You have conquered death and opened the gate of
   eternity.
Help us live today with the hope of life forever with
   You.
This we ask through Christ our Lord.

                    (An Easter prayer)

Reviewing Part One

Summary

In this Part, you have learned several truths of your Catholic faith.

1. God has created you as a special and unique person, and He wants you to be happy with Him forever.
2. God the Father is the Creator of heaven and earth, He created the world out of love, and He has entrusted this creation to people.
3. God the Father has chosen people to be His own. Through Jesus Christ, His Son, people belong to the Church, and in this community of believers, they follow the Way of Jesus.
4. The signs, or marks, of the Church are unity, apostolicity, catholicity, and holiness.
5. One of the qualities of God's love is forgiveness. He always offers people the chance to forgive and be forgiven.
6. The Holy Spirit is God the Father's gift to His People. The Spirit helps people grow in Christian love and courage.
7. Christians believe in the resurrection from the dead. By His suffering, death, and resurrection, Jesus overcame death and showed people that life goes on forever.

Questions

1. Why is it important for you to have a sense of your own identity?
2. In what three ways did Jesus show His disciples how special they were?

3. In what ways is creation a gift?
4. What are four ways to accept God's gift of love?
5. What are the four marks of the Church? Briefly describe each one.
6. What is the fourfold message of Jesus about God's forgiveness?
7. Why is forgiveness an important part of loving someone?
8. What was the promise Jesus made to His friends at the Last Supper?
9. How does the Holy Spirit help people grow and change?
10. What is the meaning of the resurrection of Jesus?

True or False

Circle the T if the statement is true. Circle the F if the statement is false.

1. The only way to discover who you are is to compare yourself to others.   T   F
2. Creation is a gift which shows you how much God your Father loves you.   T   F
3. You can show your faith in God's love for you by sharing the gift of love with others.   T   F
4. Jesus said that lepers, tax collectors, and sinners were to be considered outcasts in His Church.   T   F
5. No matter what, you should try to see the good in yourself that God your Father sees in you.   T   F
6. You can act forgiving by always telling on others when they do something wrong.   T   F
7. The gift of counsel is the ability to seek and to give help to others.   T   F

8. The gift of courage helps the followers of Jesus be
   totally unconcerned about danger.   T   F
9. Jesus was not at all afraid of suffering.   T   F
10. You are so loved by God that you will live forever. T   F

Matching

Match the item in column B which best identifies each
person in column A.

A	**B**
1. ___ Benedict Joseph Labre	a. Wanted the Second Vatican Council to help make Christians one
2. ___ Joseph Cardijn	
3. ___ Rose Hawthorne	
4. ___ Hosea	b. Started schools and hospitals for blacks and native Americans
5. ___ Perpetua	
6. ___ Pope John XXIII	c. Was so faithful to her belief in Jesus that she faced death by the sword
7. ___ Kate Drexel	
	d. Wanted young people to band together to help one another be holy
	e. Was a prophet whose love for his wife showed God's forgiveness
	f. Showed how to grow and to change in the Spirit
	g. Seemed like a failure but was a success in God's eyes

Vocabulary

Use each of the following terms in a sentence.

mission	disciples
council	piety
worship	Pharisee
homage	Orthodox

Celebration

Plan a class celebration of Christian identity. Use prayers, readings, and ideas from this Part of the book. Set aside a special time to hold this prayer service. Remember, the celebration should show how your class is special, loved by God, part of the Church, forgiven, helped by the Spirit, and meant to live forever with God. Pages 284–285 of your Handbook will help you with your plans. Be sure to include both music and actions in the service, too.

God highly exalted Him
and bestowed on Him the name above
every other name.
So that at the name of Jesus,
every knee must bend
in the heavens, on the earth,
and under the earth,
and every tongue proclaim
to the glory of God the Father:
Jesus Christ is Lord!

(Philippians 2:9–11)

PART TWO

Jesus Christ, Son of the Living God

7

Who Do You Say That I Am?

In This Chapter

You will discover who you believe Jesus Christ to be.

You will learn some of the titles the followers of Jesus have given Him over the years.

You will see how learning more about Jesus can teach you more about yourself.

A Statement of Faith

ou are special. You are loved by God the Father. You belong to the Church. You have received the Holy Spirit in Baptism. You are forgiven, and you will live forever. Those very powerful truths about you and just who you are have their source in a very important historical event—the *Incarnation*.

God had a message that was too important to trust to prophets, kings, teachers, or even angels. So, God sent Jesus to bring the message of the Father's love to everyone who would ever live. Every Christmas, in churches, on greeting cards, on television programs, in newspapers, and in shop windows, the story of the arrival of Jesus is told again.

Incarnation The teaching of the Church that God became man in Jesus. The birth of Jesus is sometimes called the mystery of the Incarnation.

In those days Caesar Augustus published a decree ordering a census of the whole world. This first census took place while Quirinius was governor of Syria. Everyone went to register, each to his own town. And so Joseph went from the town of Nazareth in Galilee to Judea, to David's town of Bethlehem—because he was of the house and lineage of David—to register with Mary, his espoused wife, who was with child.

While they were there, the days of her confinement were completed. She gave birth to her firstborn son and wrapped him in swaddling clothes and laid him in a manger, because there was no room for them in the place where travelers lodged.

(Luke 2:1–7)

Almost thirty years later, Jesus was sitting with His friends near the town of Caesarea Philippi. He asked them, "Who do people say that I am?"

The disciples were a little put off by the question, but they began to chat about the various opinions people had about the identity of Jesus. Jesus listened to their chatter for a few moments, and then, He interrupted. "But who do *you* say that I am?" Jesus asked. "You are My friends and followers. You have been with Me for a long time. What is your opinion?"

You have been a Christian for quite some time. You are identified as belonging to the Church. So, imagine that you are sitting with Jesus—the Person you follow. Using the chart below as a guide, answer the two questions Jesus asked of His disciples. First, list three answers to the question, "Who do people say that I am?" Briefly explain your answers. Then, answer the question, "Who do you say that I am?" Briefly explain that answer, too. Finally, discuss what you have done.

Questions	Answers	Explanations
1. Who do people say I am?	a. b. c.	a. b. c.
2. Who do you say I am?		

Questions

1. Why is it important for you to know and to understand the identity of Jesus?
2. What are your feelings and thoughts when you hear the Christmas story read or told?
3. Is it hard or easy for you to express how you think and feel about Jesus? Explain your answer.

Activity

Choose one of the Scripture passages listed below. Read the passage, and then, in your own words, describe what that passage teaches you about Jesus. When you have written your description, gather in small groups to talk about what you have done. Be sure to include in your group people who have read different passages.
a. Mark 10:46–52
b. Mark 1:29–31
c. Luke 23:35–43
d. John 20:24–29

Getting to Know You

Introductions are a very important part of life. While you were very young, you were taught how to make introductions and how to introduce yourself. Introductions are part of good manners—the ways people treat one another. Some introductions are very simple. They happen in the hall at school or at a party. "Judy Kramer, this is Luis Reyna. Luis Reyna, this is Judy Kramer."

Other introductions are more complicated. These kinds of introductions usually take place at formal gatherings. Maybe you have heard these more formal introductions at an assembly in school, in church on a Sunday morning, or on a television program. They go something like this: "Friends, it is my pleasure to introduce to you a woman of great learning. She is a past president of the local bank. She was a two-term state representative. She earned a master's degree from City University and has been a member of this community for her whole life. May I present our new mayor, the honorable Mrs. Clara Simpson-Brown!"

When the Apostles went out from Jerusalem, they were giving anyone who would listen an introduction to Jesus. They wanted everyone to believe in Jesus, but before these people could believe, they had to know and to understand just who this Jesus was.

Titles

In today's working world, a title often reveals what a person does for a living. For example, if someone is the president of a company, you know that this person is in charge of running the business. Titles such as lawyer, police officer, fire fighter, schoolteacher, laboratory assistant, newspaper carrier, and the like tell you something about a person, certainly, but usually only what a person does.

Knowing a person's function can help you relate to that person. Knowing what a person does can help get some conversation started. Chances are good that you would talk to an astronaut quite differently than you would to a professional tennis star.

When the first Christians asked the question, "Who is Jesus?" they often meant "What did He do?" The Apostles gave no single answer to that question. Instead, they introduced Jesus by many different titles. These titles helped the early Christians understand where Jesus fit in God's plan. It helped them begin to understand just how important Jesus is for the world. Some titles such as Prophet, High Priest, Servant of God, Lamb of God, Messiah, Son of David, and Son of Man helped the early believers connect Jesus to the important people in the history of Israel. These titles told them clearly that Jesus did the things that these people did. He spoke for God. He helped people worship and pray. He did God's will. He suffered for others. He was God's promised messenger. He was part of David's family.

Other titles such as Lord and Savior taught the people that Jesus was still working in the world. His influence was still being felt. Titles such as Word of God and Son of God introduced Jesus as someone who was always with God the Father. The chart below will help you remember some of these introductions to Jesus. It will help you find these introductions in the New Testament and will help you remember what each title means.

Title	New Testament	Meaning
Servant	Mark 8:31 Acts 3:13, 20	Jesus serves and suffers.
Lamb of God	John 1:29, 36 1 Peter 1:19	Jesus gives His life for all.
Priest	Hebrews 2:17 Hebrews 7:26–27	Jesus worships God for all.
Prophet	Luke 7:15–16 John 9:17	Jesus brings God's message.
Son of David	Mark 10:47 Mark 12:35–37	Jesus is a great leader.

Title	New Testament	Meaning
Son of Man	Matthew 13:37 Luke 19:10	Jesus is an important person.
Lord	Luke 10:1 Luke 11:39	Jesus is a holy ruler.
Messiah or Christ	Mark 8:27–30 Luke 2:11	Jesus is the one God had promised.
Savior	Matthew 1:21 John 4:42	Jesus rescues all from sin and death.
Word of God	John 1:1–18 Hebrews 1:1–13	Jesus reveals who God is.
Son of God	Mark 3:11 John 1:49	Jesus is very close to God.

Names Are Not Enough

After you have been introduced to someone, several things can happen. You may never see that person again. You may meet years later and have to be introduced again. Or, you may become friends with the person. If you do, you will want to know more and more about your friend. What you learned at the time you were introduced is just not enough.

As more and more people began to believe in Jesus and to try His Way, the early Church wanted to know more and more about Jesus. The question, "Who is Jesus?" took on a much deeper meaning. When the people came together, they would talk about Jesus. The *Church* believed from the beginning that somehow Jesus was both God and human. But it took almost 700 years for the Church to learn what that means and to teach the truth of it to everyone who wished to follow Jesus.

Church The People of God who believe in and follow Jesus. The Church is both an international organization of believers and the simple gathering of members of God's Family.

Centuries of Searching

Around the end of the first century, about the time when the Gospels were being written down, there were groups of Christians who decided that Jesus was God, but He was not human at all. They had the opinion that to be human was evil. Material things were the enemies of spiritual things. Therefore, these

Christians believed that Jesus only *seemed* to be human. He was not really born, nor did He suffer or die.

Others said that Jesus was not God. He was a great human being—the greatest ever. Yet, He was only human. God chose Jesus to do God's work, but because there is only one God, Jesus is just a very good man.

The Church talked these matters over. The leaders met and prayed. They remembered what the Apostles taught. They looked at what the faithful people believed. The leaders declared that somehow Jesus is both God and human.

In the fourth century, a Christian bishop named Arius began teaching that Jesus was the greatest of God's creatures. He was adopted by God to be His divine Son. As a result, Jesus was not quite as divine as the Father. He was not always God. He was turned into God at the resurrection. Many Christians believed in what Arius taught. They followed him. As a result, there was division among the followers of Jesus. The ones who believed what Arius taught were called Arian Christians.

Again, the Church discussed this problem. Again, the leaders met and prayed. They even held an official meeting, called a council, at the city of Nicaea, in A.D. 325. At this meeting, they declared that to be a member of the Church, a person had to believe that Jesus was truly God and truly human. The followers of Jesus who met at this meeting put together a document of beliefs which is still said at Mass today. This list of beliefs is called the Nicene Creed—the Profession of Faith.

Even after this meeting, there were many discussions about Jesus. The discussions arose because people really wanted to know about Jesus. Often, the leaders of the Church would meet and pray. They would read the Scriptures and ask the Holy Spirit to help them learn and understand. By the end of the seventh century, the Church had an answer for the question, "Who is Jesus?" The Church taught (and still teaches) that Jesus Christ is one Person who has

two natures—human and divine. These two natures are so wonderfully united in Jesus that He is truly human and truly divine. The Church even had a special Greek name for what they taught about Jesus. They called this union of two natures in one Person the *hypostatic union*.

Still Searching

Every person who loves and follows Jesus is still searching to understand more and more about Him. People pray and study. People read the Scriptures trying to find out more and more about Jesus. Some people, called *theologians*, have a vocation to spend their whole lives learning and teaching about Jesus and His Father and the Holy Spirit. These men and women pray, search, study, write, and teach. They still bring what they have learned to the Church so that the pope and the bishops can review what they have done.

You are a member of the Church. You are learning at Mass, at home, in religion class, and in your discussions with friends, just who Jesus is. You can talk to Jesus in prayer and listen to Him, too. You see, this Jesus, who is human and divine, who always was and who will be forever, who lived and suffered and died to save people, is also your Friend.

Hypostatic union The term which is used to express the fact that Jesus is both human and divine. The hypostatic union means that the one Person of Jesus Christ has two separate natures.

Theologian A person who studies and teaches about God. Theologians have a special vocation to help the followers of Jesus learn more about God, the Church, and the beliefs of the Family of God.

Questions

1. What do the different titles of Jesus teach you about Him?
2. What does the Church teach about Jesus?
3. What is your favorite title for Jesus? Why is it your favorite?
4. How can you learn more about Jesus?

Activities

1. In small groups, select one of the passages from the Bible listed below. Read the passage in the group. Then, spend a few moments in silence talking to Jesus in your heart about what you have read. Discuss what this passage teaches you about Jesus.
   a. Luke 17:25
   b. Colossians 1:15—20
   c. Matthew 27:54
   d. Luke 7:13—19
2. Listen to a recording of a song about Jesus. Choose any such song that you have available. Share what the song teaches you about Jesus. Use the song as a class prayer.

Turn Your Beliefs into Actions

Sometimes, how you act tells who you are. The members of the Church learned about Jesus by studying and praying about what He said and did. But they also learned a lot about Jesus by seeing themselves—the followers of Jesus. The more they learned about Jesus, the more they knew how to act like His followers. The more they acted like His followers, the more they learned about Jesus.

This is true because Jesus is much more than a historical event. When He was with His disciples on the night before He died, He gave them a very special message: "You are My friends. Love one another." What Jesus was telling the Apostles, He is telling everyone who believes in Him. "I love you. You can show how much you love Me by loving one another. I show My love in actions. You can show your love in actions, too."

Using the steps below as a guide, study two or three things you know about Jesus and how you can turn what you believe into caring actions for others.

1. **What Jesus did**

2. **What that teaches me about Jesus**

3. **What I learned means to me**

4. **How I can put what I learned into action**

5. **How my action shows love for others**

Review

Circle the T if the statement is true. Circle the F if the statement is false.

1. Titles teach very little about what a person does.   T   F

2. The titles of Jesus helped the Apostles introduce Jesus to people.   T   F

3. Jesus is only God, and He just appears to be human.   T   F

4. The Church has little to say about what people believe about Jesus.   T   F

5. One of the most important titles of Jesus is Friend.   T   F

Projects

1. Make a banner, poster, or bulletin-board display to show the answer to the question, "Who is Jesus?" Use the titles found in this chapter. You can use the Scripture passages, too. Try to use pictures or symbols to show what you have learned about Jesus. Perhaps, you can display what you have done where other classes or the whole parish can share it.

2. You can learn a lot about who people believe Jesus to be by the way artists have pictured Him throughout the years. Collect various pictures of Jesus from magazines, religious books, art books, and the like. Display the pictures and discuss what these pictures teach you about Jesus.

3. Share with your family the five steps of putting into action what you learn about Jesus. Maybe the family could use the steps together.

Prayer

To Jesus Christ, our sovereign King,
Who is the world's salvation,
All praise and homage do we bring
And thanks and adoration.
Christ Jesus, Victor!
Christ Jesus, Ruler!
Christ Jesus, Lord and Redeemer!

(Monsignor Martin B. Hellriegel)

8

Christ
in the Gospels

In This Chapter

You will learn the meaning of a mystery.

You will discover how the Gospels teach the mystery of Jesus.

You will see how important it is for you to read and to understand the Gospels.

I Love a Mystery

The two boys walked out of the theater just as the sun was starting to set. Jerry was waving his hands wildly. Greg was more thoughtful.

"What a great movie!" Jerry said. "I knew it was the reporter all along. For a while it looked like the state trooper was the murderer, but I kept believing the reporter did it."

"How could you be so sure?" Greg asked. "I first thought the brother-in-law did it. Then I was convinced that the drunk had done it by accident. When they found the notes in the file, I thought the newspaper publisher was the killer."

"No, no, no!" Jerry went on. "The clues were there all along. All you had to do was follow the clues. The footprints in the garden, the broken glass by the fireplace, the notes in the file, all pointed to the reporter. He was lying to both the brother-in-law *and* the state trooper."

"I was never sure who did it," Greg said, "but it really was a great movie!"

"It sure was a great movie," Jerry said.

The two boys walked all the way home discussing the twists and turns of the exciting plot.

What makes a mystery so exciting is that some of the facts are known, while some of them are hidden. To solve a mystery, the detective has to look for clues—tiny hints about what happened at the time of the crime. Then, the detective carefully puts all the clues and hints together to get a picture of what happened and who committed the crime. What makes mystery stories so much fun for the readers or the viewers is thinking along with the detective as he or she puts all the pieces together.

The early Christians often referred to Jesus as a *mystery*. While they did not mean exactly what authors like Dick Francis or P. D. James mean when

Mystery A truth that can be known only after God reveals it but which still is impossible to understand completely. The fact that Jesus is both God and human is a mystery.

they write mysteries, the early Christians did mean that they had to search for Jesus. Part of the identity of Jesus was revealed. Part of that identity was still hidden. Those who love and believe in Jesus have to follow clues and hints to get a better picture of Jesus Christ, the Son of God.

Why didn't God publish an official biography of Jesus? Well, in a way, He did—the Gospels. But because Jesus is no ordinary celebrity, the Gospels are no ordinary books. God does not just want people to *know* about His Son. He wants everyone to believe in Jesus and to follow His Way. So, the Gospels are much more like mystery books. You have to dig and search and believe to discover Jesus.

Questions

1. Why are mysteries so exciting for people?
2. What is a mystery?
3. Why are the Gospels like mystery books?
4. Have you ever followed clues to make some important discovery? What did it feel like when you made your discovery?

Activity

Many simple games are based on the reading or the understanding of visual or verbal clues. Charades, twenty questions, and daffy definitions are examples of such games. In small groups, spend a few minutes playing one such game. As a group, discuss how you followed the clues to win the game. Then, discuss times when you learn about things by following clues.

Faith in Christ Jesus

The Gospels are very special documents for the followers of Jesus. Every time you go to Mass, you hear a reading from the Gospels. The lessons and teachings of Jesus are found in the Gospels. The little that is known about the facts of His life are found in the Gospels. The names of the Apostles, the places Jesus visited, where He suffered, and how He died are all found in the Gospels.

It is important to remember that the Gospels are not Jesus' diaries or autobiographies. The Gospels are stories written by people who loved Jesus and remembered what He was like. At first, nothing much was written about the life of Jesus. Whenever believers gathered, they would talk about Jesus. The Apostles or other disciples who knew Jesus would tell about Him and share His message with the group. Usually, they were answering questions that came from the people—questions about what it meant to be a follower of Jesus. People wanted to know what made them different or special. The Apostles and other leaders used stories about Jesus or stories Jesus Himself told to help the Christians understand themselves.

How the Gospels Came to Be

Tess was studying for her music test. "Why can't I remember this stuff?" She leaned over to her friend to ask for help.

"Judy," Tess said, "you play the piano. Help me remember which notes fall on the lines of the staff and which notes fall in the spaces. I just can't seem to keep them straight."

Judy smiled. For her, remembering where the notes were was second nature. But she remembered being a very little girl and having to learn the notes for the first time. So, she eagerly helped Tess.

"Here," Judy said, "see how the notes in the spaces F, A, C, and E spell the word *face* which rhymes with *space*."

"Oh, how neat!" cried Tess. "I'll never forget that."

"Now," Judy continued, "the notes on the lines are E, G, B, D, and F. Make a little sentence with the letters. The one I learned was '*Every Good Boy Does Fine.*' Now, you should remember the notes forever."

When Jesus taught, He used some sentences over and over. He used poems, parables, stories, and catchphrases so that His hearers would remember His teaching. Remember that Jesus did not hand out sheets of paper with His message on it. He did all His teaching with words and actions. After the resurrection and the coming of the Holy Spirit, the Apostles used what they had learned from Jesus. They adapted their message to the different people and places they visited. Finally, when the eyewitnesses to Jesus' life, death, and resurrection began to die, their teaching was written down. As a result, the writings were not step-by-step, word-for-word accounts of Jesus, His words, and His actions. They were summaries of what the whole community of believers—the Church—knew and believed to be true. The Gospels also contained what the followers of Jesus considered most important. You might have lots of questions like "What did Jesus look like?" "How tall was He?" "What color was His hair?" The early believers, however, were much more concerned about His words, His stories, His actions, and the effect Jesus had on people. So, that is what got written down.

A Closer Look

When you look at each of the four Gospels, you will notice similarities and differences. The Gospels of Matthew, Mark, and Luke are rather alike. They concentrate on certain teachings and events in the life of Jesus. They even, at times, repeat the same stories. These three Gospels are called the *synoptic* Gospels. The Gospel of John is quite a bit different. It is longer and more poetic. It has some stories in it that are not found in the other Gospels.

Each of the Gospels was written by a different person for a different audience. Each of the Gospel writers listened to the Holy Spirit and wrote down very important clues to the identity of Jesus. The chart below will help you see these differences. The chart will give you some very good clues to understanding each of the Gospels.

Synoptic Holding the same or a similar view. The Gospels of Matthew, Mark, and Luke are called synoptic because they follow the same general outline.

Author	When Written	Audience	Picture of Jesus
Mark	After A.D. 70	Roman Christians	Jesus is the Christ, the Son of God. Yet, He is a real human being with feelings.
Matthew	After A.D. 85	Jewish converts	Jesus is the long-awaited Messiah. Matthew stresses how Jesus fulfills the Old Testament hopes.
Luke	After A.D. 75	Greek Christians	Jesus is a merciful Savior who identifies with the poor and the outcast. He seeks to include everyone in His kingdom.
John	After A.D. 90	Christian groups in the Middle East	Jesus is the divine messenger of the Father. He is present in the community and in the sacraments.

As you read through each of the Gospels, you discover more clues. You see that there are many different kinds of writing in the Gospels. There are parables, stories, passages from the Hebrew Scripture, prayers, and lists. Each *evangelist* used these kinds of writing to help people remember the important messages of the life of Jesus.

The Gospels also have four groupings of teachings about Jesus: (1) deeds, (2) sayings, (3) stories, or

Evangelist A term for the authors of the four Gospels. The word *evangelist* means "a bearer of good news."

narratives, and (4) speeches. The deeds of Jesus include His miracles, His travels, His baptism, His temptation in the the desert. The sayings of Jesus include discussions, short lessons, *proverbs*, rules, and parables. Stories, or narratives, about Jesus include the Christmas story, the story of His childhood, the passion, the death, and the resurrection. Finally, speeches include the longer teachings of Jesus like the Sermon on the Mount or His talk to the Apostles at the Last Supper.

If you know these classifications, you have clues as to what the Gospels meant to the early Christians and how they teach about Jesus.

Proverbs Short sayings about how the People of God should live. Jesus often used proverbs to teach the Good News of the kingdom of God.

The Living Word of God

In the first century after the death of Jesus, many stories were told, and many books and letters were written about Jesus. The leaders of the Church sifted through all the writings, letters, sermons, and narratives that were written. The leaders studied them and prayed to God for guidance. They also saw how the various writings were treated by the believers.

Finally, by the end of the fourth century, the Church taught that the four Gospels (Matthew, Mark, Luke, and John), the Acts of the Apostles, certain Epistles of Paul and other Apostles, and the Book of Revelation—twenty-seven books in all—were the official Christian Scriptures. The Church believes that these writings have the *inspiration* of the Holy Spirit and are the Living Word of God.

When you read the Gospels, you are meeting Jesus. You are following His footsteps through the early Church. You are discovering more pieces to the puzzle, more parts to the mystery. Because you are a follower of Jesus, the New Testament is your book. The Gospels are like a gift from a friend. The more you use the gift, the closer you feel and become to your Friend, Jesus Christ.

Inspiration A term used to describe how the Holy Spirit helped the writers of the Bible to write what is true. The writers worked under the guidance, or inspiration, of the Holy Spirit.

Questions

1. How are the Gospels different from biographies of Jesus?
2. What are some of the steps in the way the Gospels came to be?
3. What are some of the differences between the Gospels? Why are there differences?
4. What are some of the kinds of writing in the Gospels?
5. What is your favorite part of the Gospels? Why is it your favorite? What kind of writing is it? What does it mean to you?

Activities

1. Form four different groups. Each group can take one of the four Gospels. Then, using the picture of Jesus described in the chart on page 93, find two examples of this in the Gospel. Discuss the examples. Share what you have discovered with the whole class.
2. Pretend that you are an evangelist. The class is your audience. Write a short paragraph describing Jesus for your audience. Share the results with the whole class. If you wish, you can share the same exercise with your family.

Sharing the Gospels

T he mystery of Jesus cannot be discovered overnight. Following the clues is a process that goes on throughout a lifetime. You would be pretty shocked if your best friend came up to you after school and said, "You know, I know enough about you. I never want to learn more. So, if you don't mind, I am not going to talk to you anymore. I am not going to spend time with you anymore." You would probably consider that conversation to be the end of a friendship.

One of the reasons the Gospel is read at every Mass and the celebrant explains the Gospel is to keep the discovery process going for all the believers. It is important that the followers of Jesus always read and study the Gospels. Even though you may not understand everything all at once, you will keep in contact with Christ in the Gospels. You will keep following the clues. To practice doing just that, choose one of the passages listed below. When you have read the passage, close your eyes and think over what you have read. Talk to Jesus in your own words about what you have read. Finally, write down one or two sentences describing how what you have read has been a clue to knowing more about your Friend, Jesus.

1. Mark 10:13–16—Jesus blesses the children
2. Matthew 1:18–25—the birth of Jesus
3. Mark 6:34–44—Jesus feeds the five thousand
4. Luke 7:1–10—the cure of the servant
5. John 11:1–44—the raising of Lazarus

When you have finished, discuss what you have done. You can talk about it in small groups or with the whole class.

Review

Fill in the missing words in the following sentences.

1. The early Christians often referred to ____ as a mystery.

2. The Gospels answer questions about what it means to be a ____ of Jesus.

3. The Gospels contain what the believers considered most ____ about Jesus.

4. Parables are examples of the ____ of Jesus.

5. The Church believes that the Christian Scriptures have the ____ of the Holy Spirit.

Projects

1. For one week, set aside five minutes every day to read something from the Gospels. Each day, keep a record of what you have read—sayings, deeds, stories, sermons, and the like. At the end of the week, review what you have done and briefly write what you have learned about Jesus. Share the results of your Gospel study with the class.

2. Have a brief prayer service celebrating your discovery of the mystery of Jesus. Choose readings from the Gospels. Choose some music, too. Pages 284–285 of your Handbook will help you plan the service.

Prayer

Father, all those You gave me
I would have in My company where I am,
to see this glory of Mine which is Your gift to Me.
Just Father, the world has not known You;
and these friends have known that you sent Me.
To them I have revealed Your name,
and I will continue to reveal it so that Your love for
Me may live in them, and I may live in them.

(Prayer of Jesus, *John 17:24–26*)

9

The Good News

In This Chapter

You will discover the central message of Jesus.

You will learn why this message is called the Good News.

You will see how this Good News is a challenge for you to change and to grow.

Film at Eleven!

n every television newsroom and in the editorial offices of every newspaper, amid the bustle and clatter of machines and computers and typewriters, sits a very important person. While reporters and editors are polishing up stories and trying to meet deadlines, this person has the job of writing the *fewest* words. This person writes the headlines for the newspaper or the leading lines for the news broadcasts.

When the pile of newspapers flies off the truck and lands with a smack on the pavement, the work of the headline writer stares up from the ground: "Six Die in Valley Flood!" People passing by see that line, pick up the paper, pay the news seller, and read that story.

During a break in the evening program, a news-caster with a frantic look on his or her face, stares at the camera, and reads a lead line that is meant to keep everyone tuned in to watch the whole evening news: "Mayor resigns, and the city faces riots and ruin. Film at eleven!"

Headlines capture attention. They answer the questions, "Who?" "What?" "When?" "Why?" and "How?" And they make people want to find out the story and the details behind the headlines.

Imagine that you have just been appointed editor of the school paper. Your first job is to write three headlines for the stories listed below. Remember, you want to catch your readers' attention so that they will read the stories.

1. A story about the school basketball team which is going to the city finals.
2. A story about your appointment as editor of the paper and about your plans for the future.
3. A story about the eighth-grade religion class and what the students think about it.

Read the headlines aloud, and as a class, select the three best headlines for each story.

Questions

1. Why are headlines important in conveying news?
2. What kinds of headlines best get people's attention?
3. Which of the three headlines did you find hardest to write? easiest to write? Why?
4. What headline could you write about Jesus that would tell everyone what you believe about Him?

Activity

Choose one of the speeches listed below. Each of them was made by Saint Peter after the coming of the Holy Spirit. Then, write one head-line which you feel best summarizes the speech. Talk about the readings in small groups.
a. Acts 2:14–30
b. Acts 4:8–12
c. Acts 13:16–41

Everyone Loves Good News

People today are news crazy. Everybody wants to know what is going on in the world. When a plane crashes, when a president speaks, when a team wins a championship, when a big building burns to the ground, cameras and reporters are there. More people saw Pope John Paul II celebrate Midnight Mass on television last Christmas than ever saw Jesus or the Apostles or the first fifty popes all put together. This is an age when news happens instantly. But things were different at the time of Jesus.

At the time of Jesus, almost every bit of news was handed on by word of mouth. Teachers and messengers would stand in a public place—usually by a well or near the market—and shout the news. Jesus told His Apostles to spread the word of His teaching to all nations. After Jesus returned to His Father, the Apostles set about the task of telling everyone about the new Way of Jesus. The Holy Spirit gave them the courage to share in public what they had experienced with Jesus. They shouted the headlines to anyone who would listen.

The headlines the Apostles used contained the very heart of the Christian faith. This core was called the *kerygma*, the Good News of Jesus. The headlines of the Good News usually contained four very special ideas.

1. Jesus is the Christ—the Messiah promised by God.
2. Jesus died to take away people's sins.
3. Jesus rose again from the dead.
4. Jesus is with the Father and will put in a good word for everyone—He will continue to care.

Wherever the Apostles went, they spread the Good News by proclaiming these headlines.

Kerygma The Good News of salvation. The word *kerygma* means "good news." The teaching of the Apostles after Pentecost is called the kerygma.

Answering Questions

Just as you are interested in reading or watching
news stories that are going to affect your life, the
people who listened to the Apostles were very interested in the headlines they heard: "Jesus, who was
crucified, has risen from the dead!" "Jesus, the
Nazorean, gave Himself up for your sins!" When the
people heard the headlines, they had many questions
about Jesus. They wanted to hear more about the
Man who had beaten sin and death—two of their
worst enemies.

At first, people asked for a few facts: Where did He die? How did He die? Where was He from? When was He born? Who were His family and friends?

The preaching of the Apostles contained a few of the answers to the factual questions. Jesus was born in Bethlehem. He grew up in Nazareth. Joseph was His father's name, and His mother's name was Mary. James Joseph, Simon, and Jude were His close relatives. Jesus spoke Aramaic and Hebrew.

About the age of thirty, Jesus began to travel and to teach. First, He was baptized by John the Baptizer. He gathered some disciples around Himself. He associated with all kinds of people. He healed people and did other signs and wonders to show His care.

After a time, Jesus got into trouble with the authorities. He was captured, He suffered, and He was put to death. He was buried in a borrowed grave, but three days later, He rose from the dead. After spending a few weeks encouraging His disciples, Jesus returned to be with His Father.

After the people learned a few facts about Jesus, they wanted to ask more personal questions: What was He like? What was His message? How did He teach? What did He do? What does He want us to do? How can we be like Him? Over the years, the Apostles answered those questions. The answers were talked over and shared, and (as you learned in the last chapter) the answers were finally written down in the Gospels.

A Gospel Tour

It is important for you to know your way around the Gospels if you are going to be a faithful follower of Jesus. At some time, you should read each Gospel through from beginning to end. When you do, the charts on page 104 will help you find your way through each of the Gospels. Matthew, Mark, and Luke have very similar plans. The Gospel of John has a special plan all its own. These two charts can be like a blueprint for you to follow through each Gospel as you read it.

Plan of the Gospel	Matthew	Mark	Luke
Opening	*1:1—4:11* a. Jesus' family b. Birth c. Baptism d. Temptation	*1:1–13* a. Baptism b. Temptation	*1:1—4:13* a. Birth b. Baptism c. Jesus' family d. Temptation
Ministry	*4:12—13:58* a. Call of disciples b. Sermon on Mount c. Miracles d. Parables e. Conflict	*1:14—6:13* a. Call of disciples b. Miracles c. Parables d. Conflict	*4:14—9:50* a. Call of disciples b. Great Sermon c. Miracles d. Parables e. Transfiguration
Journeys	*14:1—20:34* a. Death of John b. Miracles c. Prediction of the passion d. Transfiguration e. Journey to Jerusalem	*6:14—10:52* a. Death of John b. Miracles c. Prediction of the passion d. Transfiguration e. Journey to Jerusalem	*9:51—21:38* a. Journey to Jerusalem b. Miracles c. Parables d. Rich young man e. Zacchaeus f. Entering the city
Passion, death, and resurrection	*21:1—28:20* a. Entering the city b. Last Supper c. Trial d. Crucifixion e. Resurrection f. Sending out the Apostles	*11:1—16:20* a. Entering the city b. Last Supper c. Trial d. Crucifixion e. Resurrection f. Sending out the Apostles	*22:1—24:53* a. Last Supper b. Trial c. Crucifixion d. Resurrection

Plan of the Gospel	John
Opening	*1:1–18*—Jesus is the Word of God.
Book of signs	*1:19—12:50*—Jesus does God's work. a. Call of the disciples b. Miracles c. Speeches d. Raising of Lazarus from the dead
Book of God's glory	*13:1—20:31*—Jesus shows God's great love. a. Last Supper b. Prayer of Jesus c. Passion and crucifixion d. Resurrection

When you take a tour of the Gospels, you are hearing the Good News and are going beyond the headlines. You are discovering what you are to be if you are a follower of Jesus. You are reminded that your Father loves you so much that He sent Jesus to show you how to live and how to love others—how to be the best *you* possible.

Questions

1. What were the Apostles most interested in sharing with people when they talked about Jesus?
2. What term describes the headlines the Apostles used?
3. What were the four special ideas in the headlines the Apostles used?
4. Why is it important to know more than the headlines of the Good News?

Activities

1. In small groups, choose one of the Gospel outlines given in this chapter. Working with a copy of the New Testament, find the beginning and the end of each section. Then, find examples of each of the items mentioned in the outline. Work carefully, and discuss your searching while you are doing it. It might take your group almost thirty minutes to do this activity well.

2. Choose one of the events in the life of Jesus which are listed below. Then, compare how the story is told in each of the Gospels. Why do you think there are some differences? What you learned in chapter 8 might help you with your answer.
   a. Baptism of Jesus— Matthew 3:13—17, Mark 1:9—11, Luke 3:21—22, John 1:32—34.
   b. Jesus walks on water—Matthew 14:22—23, Mark 6:45—52, John 6:16—21.
   c. The loaves and fishes—Matthew 14:13—21, Mark 6:32—44, Luke 9:10—17, John 6:1—13.

A Living Gospel

hile news is a very important part of daily life, you do not learn math from the newspaper or the six o'clock news. While you may use television and records in school, you also have teachers, textbooks, libraries, and other resources to help you with the serious business of learning. It takes time to learn how to read, how to express yourself, how to do math, and to develop the other skills you need to get along in your world. The same is true in learning about Jesus and how you can follow Him.

You may be the only Gospel someone ever reads. As a follower of Jesus, the Gospels are your books. The skills you learn from reading the Gospels are the skills of believing, hoping, and loving. When you learn the Gospels and share with others what the Gospels teach, people will see what Jesus is all about by looking at you.

The Gospels are a challenge for you to grow and to change. Read the Gospel headlines listed below. Using the chart as a guide, briefly describe what you think is the story behind the headlines. Then, describe how you can make that challenging story your own. Discuss what you have written in class. Decide how you as a class can support one another in becoming a living Gospel.

Headline	The Story	The Challenge
1. God Sends Son to Earth!		
2. Jesus Feeds 5,000!		
3. Jesus Forgives Sinner!		
4. Jesus Crucified!		
5. Jesus' Tomb Found Empty!		

Review

Match the item in column B which best describes
each item in column A.

A	B
1. ___ Kerygma	a. Loving, hoping, and believing
2. ___ Headlines	b. Putting the Good News into action
3. ___ Living Gospel	c. The core of the Good News
4. ___ Knowing the Gospels	d. Getting the attention of the listeners
5. ___ Gospel skills	e. Discovering the Good News

Projects

1. Collect headlines from the newspaper, or record
   leadlines from the evening news. Make a poster
   or banner using the headlines. In addition, put
   on the poster or banner headlines from the
   Gospels which give messages of belief, hope,
   and love to the people who read the news stories.

2. Using the stories listed below, continue the work
   you began in this part of the chapter. First, write
   a headline for the story. Then, describe the
   story in your own words. Finally, describe the
   challenge you find in the story.
   a. The healing of the leper—Matthew 8:2–4
   b. The cure of the servant—Luke 7:1–10
   c. The cure of the blind man—Mark 10:46–52
   d. Calming the Storm—Matthew 8:23–27
   e. The cure of Jairus's daughter—Luke 8:40–42

3. Make up a prayer service on the kerygma, or the
   Good News. Use thoughts and readings found in
   this chapter. Pages 284–285 of your Handbook
   will help you with your plans.

Prayer

May the Lord be on my lips, in my heart,
   and on my mind,
so that I may read this Holy Gospel with hope,
   with love, and with faith.

(Prayer before reading the Gospels)

10

Jesus in Action

In This Chapter

You will discover how people who love Jesus put His words into action.

You will learn some very important needs people have.

You will use a special recipe for putting Jesus into action in your life.

Louise and Vincent

he black caped figure leaned into the wind and rain. The Paris winter of 1633 was a bitter one. The bearded man pushed his face into the weather to get his bearings. He saw the lamp in the window of the house across the street. He ran a bit to get to the door. "Thud, thud," went the door knocker. Immediately, the door opened. "Madam is expecting you, Father Vincent. Go right into the drawing room," the servant said.

Seconds later, Father Vincent and Louise de Marillac were kneeling before the crucifix. After a few moments of prayer, Father Vincent de Paul got to his feet. He began pacing around the room, his fingers frequently poking the air to make a point. "Too many poor in Paris," he began. "We cannot seem to keep up."

Father Vincent paused for a breath and then continued, "I have eighty brothers in the Congregation for the Mission. I have thirty-seven gray ladies who volunteer every day to visit the sick, carry food to the hungry, and round up orphan children from the streets, but more is needed."

"Father," Louise said trying to get the man's attention, "I have an idea which just might . . ."

"We must not have just a *feeling* love for people," Vincent continued, unaware for the moment that Louise was trying to make a point. "Jesus taught a *doing* love," Vincent said. "If I say I love someone, but my actions do not show that I love, then I am just what Saint Paul said—a tinkling brass or a sounding cymbal . . ."

"Father!" cried Louise. The priest paused. He realized that Louise had been trying to get his attention. He slumped into a chair, folded his fingers in front of his mouth, and prepared to listen.

"I hardly think anyone will accuse you of being a sounding cymbal," Louise went on. "But you need help in your mission. I think that the time has come for some of the gray ladies to stop being volunteers. It is time for us to become an order of sisters who spend all our time caring for the poor of Paris—and the world for that matter. We could form a community, take *religious vows,* and care for the poor."

Father Vincent became lost in thought. "Women have never done that before," Vincent replied. "It is very different. Sisters have always stayed in *cloisters.* They teach perhaps. Occasionally they have cared for the sick, but this is something very, very new."

Louise de Marillac let a big smile break across her face. "But, Monsieur Vincent, it is also very, very needed."

That afternoon, the Daughters of Charity were born. Louise de Marillac and Vincent de Paul wanted so much to make Jesus real for the poor of Paris and the world that they would let nothing stand in their way. Over the years, Vincent would remind the members of his society of priests and brothers as well as the Sisters of Charity why they had come together.

"We must care for the poor," he would say, "console them, help them, and support their cause. Since Christ willed to be born poor, He chose for Himself disciples who were poor. He made Himself the servant of the poor and shared their poverty. He went so far as to say that He would consider every deed which helps or harms the poor as done for or against Himself."

Religious vows Public promises made to God. People who have a vocation to religious life make vows of poverty, chastity, and obedience.

Cloister A special place in the houses of religious men and women which is closed to outsiders. Cloisters provide the privacy sisters and brothers need for prayer and study.

Questions

1. Why was Monsieur Vincent so anxious to care for the poor?
2. How did Louise de Marillac plan to help him with his mission?
3. Describe a time when you helped someone who needed your help. How did you feel?

Activities

1. Make a Vincent and Louise Award. Select a person or organization in your parish that is really putting faith in Jesus into action by helping the poor. Write a scroll or certificate from your class to that person or organization. On the certificate, tell how your class appreciates what is being done.
2. Read Matthew 25:31–46. When you have finished, use your own experience to write three answers to the question, "Lord, when did we see You?" Share your answers with the class.

The Kingdom of God

Jesus was never satisfied. He came to earth to bring the message of God's love. But Jesus wanted every person to benefit from that message. He was very anxious for the Good News to spread. The people of Jesus' time were painfully aware that the governments and kingdoms of the world often took advantage of people, took away their rights, made people slaves, and treated people like dirt.

Jesus taught that God's kingdom was different. God does not run things like people do. In human kingdoms, people fight to get power, but in God's kingdom, people become like little children—simple and honest. In human kingdoms, people sometimes cheat or lie to get ahead. In God's kingdom, however, sincerity and honesty are rewarded. In human kingdoms, the rich have it easy and can have anything they want. But in God's kingdom, what is in a person's heart is more important than what is in the purse.

Just as human kingdoms are often filled with wars, injustice, and mistrust, God's kingdom is to be filled with peace, justice, and love. Furthermore, Jesus insisted that God's kingdom was starting now and would keep building and growing forever. Nobody could stop it.

In His teachings and in the way He treated people, Jesus showed how members of the kingdom of God should act. Jesus showed how to respond to the needs of others. The Jewish people had a great tradition of taking care of the poor—orphans, widows, strangers, poor neighbors, debtors, and slaves. The Torah had very strong laws and customs protecting the rights and property of people. Jesus praised those laws and those customs. He did not want to change those laws. He wanted to expand them to reach out to anyone who had needs. To belong to God's kingdom, people had to meet the needs of the hurt, the hungry, the thirsty, the imprisoned, the sick, the naked, the old, the young, and even of their enemies. In short, the followers of Jesus had to work hard to make God's kingdom real.

Peace on Earth

Pope John XXIII was working feverishly at his huge wooden desk. Open on his desk was a book of the Gospels. In front of him were piles and piles of lined paper. The old pope would flip through his notes crossing out a word here or adding a word there. Every once in a while he would pick up the Gospels. He would turn the pages tenderly. Sometimes he would linger over a passage. At other times, he would page quickly ahead to find a familiar phrase and read it again. Then, the pope would shift in his chair and go back to his notes.

Almost two thousand years had gone by since Jesus announced that the kingdom of God was at hand. Through the pope's mind raced images of the successes and failures of Christians in working for the kingdom—successes and failures in putting Jesus into action. "So many needs,..." said the pope under his breath. "So many needs."

Finally, the old man put down his pen. He put the notes together in a pile and said a short prayer of thanksgiving. The work of months was finished. He had had the help and advice of many experts, but the final job had been his. In front of him on the desk was a very important *encyclical* letter to the Church. The letter was entitled *Peace on Earth*. In that letter, Pope John wanted to pull the teachings of Jesus into modern times. He wanted people to see the needs that Christians should be meeting now. He wanted everyone to know that human beings have rights, and where those rights are being hurt, God's kingdom is failing.

In his letter, Pope John listed some very basic human rights. It is important for the followers of Jesus to know these rights. They belong to everyone. They are gifts from a loving Father.

Encyclical   A letter written by the pope to bishops all around the world. Encyclicals teach many truths of the Catholic Faith and encourage people to stay faithful to God.

1. The right to life and a decent standard of living.
2. The right to respect and a good reputation.
3. The right to the freedom to search for and express truth.
4. The right to pursue art and culture.
5. The right to be informed truthfully about events.
6. The right to education and training.
7. The right to worship God according to one's conscience.
8. The right to choose freely a state of life.
9. The right to work and to work without force.
10. The right to good working conditions.
11. The right to just wages for one's work.
12. The right to private property.
13. The right to meet together and to associate with people.
14. The right to move about freely.
15. The right to take active part in public affairs.
16. The right to legal protection for all a person's rights.

What Jesus taught and what Pope John XXIII wrote about in his letter has meaning right in your parish, in your classroom, and in your home. If you are going to put Jesus into action, you have to start where you are today. The rights Pope John described belong to everyone. And they are fulfilled in the way Christians treat other people, even the people closest to them—family and friends.

Questions

1. What are some of the differences between most human kingdoms and the kingdom Jesus announced?
2. How can a person put the words of Jesus into action?
3. What was the message in Pope John XXIII's letter, Peace on Earth?
4. How can you respect the rights of people in your home, class, parish, and neighborhood?

Activities

1. Many of Jesus' parables teach about God's kingdom. These parables give hints about how the message of Jesus can be put into action. Choose three of the parables listed below, read them, and describe in your own words the message of each story.
   a. The sower—Matthew 13:3–23
   b. The weeds—Mark 13:37–43
   c. The mustard seed—Luke 13:20–21
   d. The dragnet—Matthew 13:47–50
   e. The seed—Mark 4:26–29
2. In small groups, select three of the sixteen rights from Peace on Earth. For each of the rights you have chosen, discuss ways the right can be protected and the ways in which the right can be threatened.

Recipe for Action

ven though Jesus gave the Apostles the basic ingredients for putting His words into action, people have been trying for centuries to put those ingredients together in the way they treat one another. Many times, people have failed to see the needs in the world. Sometimes, people have just neglected to care for one another. But there have always been people who were trying their best to fill their world with the teachings of Jesus.

Recently, an American bishop wrote a letter to the people in his *diocese*. In that letter, he offered a recipe for action.

Diocese A specific area in the Church usually under the leadership of a bishop. A diocese includes all the Catholic people and parishes in the area.

Recipe for Christian Action

1. Take the teachings of Jesus.
2. Blend in the needs of others.
3. Add a generous portion of self.
4. Stir with prayer and mutual support.

Yield: A better and more Christlike community.
Serves: A family, a neighborhood, a parish, a county, a state, a country, a whole world!

Using the sample recipe card below, make your own recipe. Use the actual words of Jesus and real needs in your family, school, or neighborhood. Finally, say just what of yourself you can give.

Personal Recipe for Action

1.
2.
3.
4.
Yield:
Serves:

Review

Match the action in column B which best fits each
of the rights, or needs, listed in column A.

A	B
1. ___ Right to respect	a. Sarah never runs anybody down.
2. ___ Right to life	b. Ron and Cindy take the children from the special education class to the museum.
3. ___ Right to education	c. Frances tutors in math twice a week.
4. ___ Right to art and culture	d. On Fridays after school, Andy and Jack meet to talk about current events.
5. ___ Right be to informed	e. Maxine wears a small rose to show her stand against abortion.
6. ___ Right to private property	f. Jillian volunteers to watch everybody's handbag during the volleyball game.

Projects

1. Begin a "Peace on Earth" scrapbook. Bring in articles or pictures to show each of the rights Pope John XXIII mentioned. Then, add words from the Gospels, pictures from magazines, and symbols to show how these rights can be protected.

2. Choose one of the Gospel stories listed below and rewrite it as if it were happening today. Perhaps you could act out the story for the class.
   a. Luke 16:19–31—the rich man and Lazarus
   b. Luke 10:25–37—the Good Samaritan
   c. Matthew 25:31–40—the sheep and the goats

Prayer

The Spirit of the Lord is upon me;
   therefore He has anointed me.
He has sent me to bring glad tidings to the poor,
   to proclaim liberty to captives,
Recovery of sight to the blind,
   and release to prisoners,
To announce a year of favor from the Lord.

(Luke 4:18–19)

11

One Flock, One Shepherd

In This Chapter

You will discover the kind of leadership Jesus chose for His followers.

You will see how the Apostles and their successors have kept the teachings of Jesus alive.

You will learn how to follow and how to lead in the Church of Christ.

Feed My Lambs

eter rubbed the traces of bread and fish from his beard. This had indeed been a strange morning so far. In fact, Peter's whole life seemed to be getting stranger and stranger. But right now, Peter did not know what to feel.

Just days ago, Peter had denied Jesus. He went through the bitter sorrow of knowing that the Master had been killed. Then, on that third day, when he saw Jesus again, he had been so happy he could have split in two. That was just how he felt this morning when he stumbled out of the fishing boat to find Jesus cooking breakfast on the shore. But Peter was also a little sad—a little uncertain.

Just then, Peter saw the Master's eyes. They were focused right on his. "Simon, son of John, do you love Me more than these do?" Jesus asked.

Peter swallowed hard and answered, "Yes, Lord, You know I love You."

"Feed My lambs," Jesus said.

Peter began to relax. That question had taken him by surprise. But before Peter could get comfortable again, Jesus asked, "Simon, son of John, do you love Me?"

What could the Master want? "Yes, Lord," Peter replied, "You know that I love You."

"Tend My sheep," Jesus said.

Everything around the fire was very quiet now. The other Apostles were no longer chatting among themselves. All eyes were on Simon Peter. Peter could feel the color rising in his face.

Just then, Jesus asked a third time, "Simon, son of John, do you love Me?"

Now Peter was hurt. He loved Jesus very much. He couldn't remember ever having loved anybody more. But why did Jesus have to keep asking that same question over and over again? After only a second, Peter blurted out, "Lord, You know everything. You know well that I love You!" Tears began to well up in Peter's eyes.

With that, Jesus reached over and touched Peter on the arm, looked him in the eyes, and said, "Feed My sheep!"

All at once, Peter began to remember details. He remembered the sunny morning when they had walked through the grazing sheep, and Jesus had said, "I am the good shepherd." Peter recalled the very frightening day at Caesarea Philippi when Jesus had said to him, "You are Peter, the Rock, and on this rock I will build My Church."

Peter looked again at Jesus. "I guess I have quite a job to do," Peter thought, "quite a job to do!"

Questions

1. What kinds of feelings was Peter having? Why do you think his feelings were a little confused?
2. What was the job Peter was being given to do?
3. How do you feel when you are given a special responsibility? How do you act?

Activities

1. Read the three incidents which are mentioned in this story (John 21:1—19, John 10:1—18, and Matthew 16:13—20). After reading these passages, write a brief job description for Peter. Put in your own words what you think he would be expected to do for the followers of Jesus.
2. Pretend that you are sitting at the breakfast table with Jesus, and He asks you the same question He asked Peter. Write a short paragraph answering the question. Give an example or two to show what you mean.

Servant of the Servants of God

eadership is a real gift. Not everybody can be a leader because leading others takes special gifts and talents. But in every society, leaders are very important. They help people get things done. They organize, focus, teach, command, supervise, and check progress.

You experience many different kinds of leadership in your life. Your parents give you one kind of leadership—they care for you, give you rules to follow, and they make sure that you are growing and learning in the ways you should. Teachers lead you. They make sure that you listen in class, do your homework, pass your tests, and help your classmates learn. You also experience leadership in your games and clubs. Certain people help your teams play well. They may be official "captains" or just people with the ability to pull a team or a club together.

When Jesus was on earth, He was the leader of a small band of people who wanted to be like Him. Jesus gathered these people together. He taught them about the Father. He gave them an example of how to live and to act. He trained His Apostles to be leaders and teachers, too. But Jesus taught a very special kind of leadership. He taught the Apostles that to be leaders of the People of God, they had to put all personal power out of their minds. The leaders in God's Family were to be servants—people who took care of the needs of others.

Jesus chose Peter to be the leader of the leaders. So, you could say that Peter became the servant of the servants. As a matter of fact, that is one of the titles the pope uses to this day. It is the pope's special job to make sure that the People of God have everything they need to follow Jesus.

A Little History

During the first twenty or thirty years after Jesus returned to the Father, the Apostles did a lot of traveling. They used the Roman roads and the Greek shipping routes to get to places where they could spread the Good News. In these centers, they organized groups of Christians. They chose good people to lead the groups, and then, the Apostles would move on to another place.

At first, the organization was a very loose one. Peter, James, John, Paul, and the others would keep contact with the groups they had formed by mail or by occasional visits. They would encourage the leaders, who were called bishops, to keep faithful to the teachings of Jesus and to act like loving followers of the Lord.

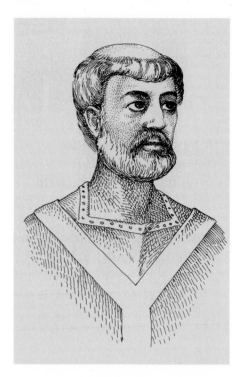

During his travels, Peter finally journeyed to Rome, the capital of the Empire. There, he formed a strong group of believers. There, Peter gave up his life for Jesus and the flock.

As a result, the group of Christians in the other centers looked to the group in Rome for leadership. After all, Rome was Peter's place, and Peter was the Rock Jesus had chosen. The bishop who took Peter's place, a very holy man named Linus, was looked upon as carrying on Peter's job. The bishops in the other centers looked to the bishop of Rome as a father.

Other cities were important for the Church, too— Antioch in Syria, Alexandria in Egypt, Jerusalem, and later Constantinople in Turkey. The bishops in these large places helped to organize the other bishops in the area. These cities became known as *patriarchates* and were very important in the growth of Christianity. But these bishops always looked to the bishop of Rome, or pope, for leadership and guidance. Things did not always run smoothly. There were often arguments and disagreements. At times, bishops broke away from the bishop of Rome. But the bishop of Rome was always honored as first and most important.

Patriarchates Very important cities in the growth of the Christian Church. The bishops who are in charge of these cities are called patriarchs. Rome, Constantinople, Alexandria, Jerusalem, and Antioch are patriarchates.

Saint Peter has had 265 successors down through the years. Some of these men have been very holy. Some have been strong and wonderful leaders. Some, however, have not been as good. Some have gotten too concerned about money or power. Others got all wrapped up in art or culture or politics, but every one of those 265 bishops of Rome have known that it was his job to care for the whole Church—to teach and to care.

Faithful to the Truth

At the Last Supper, Jesus had prayed that people would learn the truth through the Apostles. So, the Apostles saw it as their duty to spread the truth about Jesus and to keep people faithful to that truth. The Apostles discussed and shared what they learned. They checked up on one another to make sure that they believed in and lived the truth.

That tradition continues to this day. The pope and the bishops serve God's People by teaching and by sharing the truths of the faith. Sometimes, they meet together in *synods* or in *councils* to discuss the teachings of the faith and how those teachings can be shared. The pope together with the bishops share the job of holding the Gospels and traditions of the Church before the eyes of all believers.

The pope and the bishops know that the Holy Spirit is guiding the people. The pope and bishops have a very special gift. Over the years, this gift has been called *infallibility*. Many people misunderstand what infallibility is. First of all, this gift is not magic. It does not mean that everything the pope or councils say is automatically correct. Instead, this gift is the unbending faith that the Holy Spirit will not let God's People stray very far from the truth. It is the trust that the Holy Spirit will take special care that the people with responsibility in the Church will not lie or be mistaken about what all Church members are to believe and what all members are to do.

Synods and councils Meetings of members of the Church at which matters of teaching and behavior are discussed.

Infallibility The teaching of the Catholic Church that the Holy Spirit will help the pope and the bishops, when they join the pope, from being wrong when they teach about faith or morals. The pope is infallible when he speaks out as the representative of Jesus Christ on matters of faith.

Meeting Human Needs

The pope and the bishops are not just concerned about what is taught in religion class, what is preached on Sundays, how Mass is celebrated, or how the sacraments are administered. The servants of the Church are also very concerned about the world in which Christians live and work. The pope and the bishops do not forget about people who are not Catholics. They know that God loves each human being. The popes and bishops can do no less.

So, down through history, the popes have spoken out about the world, the rights of people, the problems which face society, and the dangers of selfishness. This speaking and teaching about the world is often called the Church's social teaching. In the last one hundred years, popes and the bishops, too, have taken a very strong stand on the needs of the world.

In 1891, Pope Leo XIII wrote an encyclical letter on the dignity of every human person. In this letter, he said that the rights of the person are more important that the rights of governments or companies or the rich. In 1931, Pope Pius XI wrote a letter condemning the people who got rich by taking away the rights of the poor and the workers of the world. He said that every human being is important and that people are not just tools for making a few people rich.

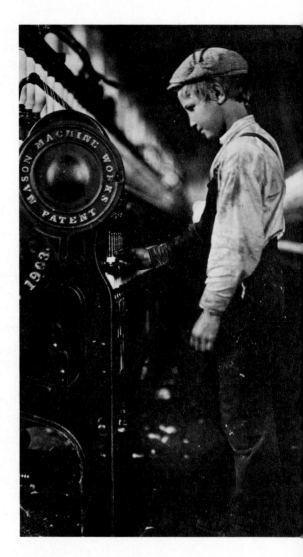

In 1961, Pope John XXIII wrote a letter called *Mother and Teacher* in which he asked all Catholics to do whatever they could to bring justice into the world. He reminded people that Jesus was a person of justice, peace, hope, and truth. Those were the qualities that Catholics were to bring to their jobs, their friendships, and their countries.

In 1981, Pope John Paul II wrote a letter to workers all over the world. It is entitled *On Human Work*. The pope defended workers. He praised them for the good they do. He told everyone that workers have a right to fair wages, medical benefits, and good conditions. They have the right to happiness and time for themselves so that they can enjoy their families and worship their God.

Vicar of Christ

When Peter listened to Jesus that morning on the shores of the lake, He understood something very important. He understood that Jesus wanted him to take His place. Peter understood that he was to feed the followers of Jesus—the flock. But over the years, Peter and the other bishops of Rome have learned that the followers of Jesus are hungry for more than bread. They are hungry for the truth, so the leaders must help people seek truth. They are hungry for faith, so the leaders try to strengthen people in faith. They are hungry for peace, so the leaders try to make the world a better place in which to live. They are hungry for justice, so the pope and bishops speak out for the rights of all the people.

Most of all, the Holy Father pulls the People of God together. He wants to make sure that the prayer of Jesus may someday come true: "O Father most holy, protect them with Your name which You have given Me that they may be one, even as We are one. So shall the world know that You sent Me, and that You love them as You love Me" *(John 17:11, 23)*.

Questions

1. What kind of leaders did Jesus want for His Church?
2. Why was the bishop of Rome so important for the believers?
3. What are some of the duties of the pope and the bishops?
4. How important are the pope and the bishops for you? Explain your answer.

Activities

1. In small groups, select one of the Scripture passages listed below. Read the passage and discuss how this passage teaches the meaning of leadership in the People of God.
   a. 1 Timothy 3:1–14— the qualities of leaders
   b. Acts 6:1–7—meeting community needs
   c. Matthew 18:1–18— become like little children
2. Today, the pope is very visible in the world. He can fly from country to country and can appear on television. Write a short paragraph on what you feel is the importance of the pope in the world today.

Follow the Leader

 As a Catholic Christian, you are part of a worldwide organization. But you experience that organization in your home, in your parish, and with your friends. Using the chart below as a guide, list three qualities of a good leader and three qualities of a good follower. Then, describe how you can use those qualities to be a good Catholic Christian at home, in your parish, and with your friends. Discuss what you have done in class. Select what the whole class considers the most important qualities of leaders and followers, and plan how the class can show these qualities.

Qualities	Home	Parish	Friends
Leader			
a.			
b.			
c.			
Follower			
a.			
b.			
c.			

Review

Circle the T if the statement is true. Circle the F if the statement is false.

1. Leadership is not very important in the People of God.   T   F

2. The leaders in God's Family are to be servants.   T   F

3. The bishop of Rome became important because Rome was the largest city in the world.   T   F

4. The pope and the bishops help people stay
   faithful to the truth.   T   F

5. The pope has no right speaking about anything
   but religion.   T   F

Projects

1. Read the story of the talents (Matthew 25:14–30
   or Luke 19:11–27) and Saint Paul's teaching
   about the Body of Christ (Romans 12:3–21). After
   the reading, write a personal statement of faith
   in which you list ways you can use your gifts to
   be a servant to God's People in your home, at
   school, in your parish, and with your friends.

2. Make a "Servant of the Servants" bulletin-board
   display. Use pictures, headlines, articles from
   magazines or the diocesan newspaper, and your
   artwork to show what leadership in the Church
   means.

3. Appoint a committee to find out how the Church
   in your diocese is run. Find out who the
   bishop is, who his principal helpers are, what
   committees and groups in the diocese help
   the bishop, and what some special projects in
   the diocese are. Discuss the findings of the
   committee.

Prayer

Eternal Shepherd, look with favor upon Your flock.
Safeguard and shelter it forevermore through John
Paul II whom You have called to shepherd the
whole Church. We ask this through our Lord
Jesus Christ who lives and reigns with You in the
unity of the Holy Spirit for ever and ever. Amen.

(Prayer from the Mass for the Holy Father)

12

Jesus Is Alive!

In This Chapter

You will recall how important it is for people who care about one another to keep in contact.

You will learn how Jesus is alive and present in the world.

You will discover how to celebrate and to share the presence of Jesus.

Keeping in Contact

t hurts to be separated from someone you love. People who care about one another really want to be together, and so it is only natural to be sad at moments of separation. Some separations are bearable because they are short. Mother goes away for a few days on business. Your best friend goes to camp for two weeks. Your brother goes to spend a month with your grandparents in Oregon. You miss the person who is away, but you know he or she will be back soon.

Some separations are harder to take. Your best friend moves across the country. Your family moves, and you have to leave school, relatives, friends, and neighbors behind. Some families experience divorces and separations, and the children of those families feel a very special sense of loss or loneliness.

Death is the biggest separation of all. People know so little about death. When a parent or a relative or a friend dies, it hurts very much. It seems like the hole that is left will never be filled.

People who care about one another try to keep in contact, even when they have to be separated. They try to fill in the feelings of loneliness with reminders of the friendship and love they have shared. Some people give gifts as reminders. "Think of me when you wear this," is the message behind the gift. Others are great letter writers. They send notes and cards to their absent friends or relatives. The notes make contact and cut down the distance between people.

Pictures and souvenirs help people keep in contact, too. Of course, telephone calls become very important. It is really exciting to get a call from a friend or relative you have not seen for a while. The points of contact between people who have to be

apart become very important for keeping the relationship alive.

Imagine for a moment that you and your best friend are going to be separated starting next week for one full year. Make plans on just how you and your friend will stay in contact over that year. Be very specific in your plans. Only one thing is not allowed—visits! Write out your plans. When you have finished, share you plans with the rest of the class.

Questions

1. Why is it so important for people to keep in contact?
2. Why is death the hardest separation to take?
3. Describe a time when you experienced a separation or a death. How did you act? How did you feel?

Activities

1. Choose one of the following openings from the Epistles of Saint Paul. Read the passage and discuss how Saint Paul felt about keeping in contact with the groups of believers.
   a. Romans 1:8—15
   b. Ephesians 1:1—7
   c. Philippians 1:3—11
   d. 2 Timothy 1:1—8
2. Visit a greeting-card store. Read through some of the messages on greeting cards which are designed to make contact with an absent friend or relative. Jot down a few of the lines, bring your notes to class, and discuss what ideas are expressed on these cards. How do they help people keep in contact?

I Am with You Always

On the night before He died, Jesus gathered His disciples around Him. The meal He shared with them that night was very special. "Whenever you do this," Jesus said, "do it as a remembrance of Me." Though the Apostles were very sad at the thought of Jesus dying and leaving, they were beginning to understand that Jesus had to leave.

After Jesus rose from the dead, the Apostles were very excited. Jesus had beaten death. This meant that they, too, were someday going to be with Jesus forever. But when Jesus left to be with His Father, there was still some sadness on the part of His followers. The Apostles knew of the Holy Spirit and His coming. They were also aware of Jesus' promise to them, "Know that I am with you until the end of the world." Gradually, they began to realize that Jesus had not gone away. Instead, He was with them in a new way.

Since the days of the Apostles, the Church has realized that Jesus is still alive and present. His friends have recognized Him everywhere. The way Jesus is present and alive now is somewhat of a mystery, but traditionally, believers have described four ways in which Jesus is alive and active in the world.

1. Jesus is present in the hearts of believers and can be contacted in prayer.
2. Jesus is present in the Gospels and can be contacted by reading the Gospels and by watching those who live the Gospels.
3. Jesus is present in the Church, His Body, and can be contacted by the faith and love shared among His members.
4. Jesus is present in the Holy Eucharist and the other sacraments, and can be contacted in the

celebration of Mass, devotion to the Blessed Sacrament, and reception of the sacraments.

The Interior Castle

Teresa sat at the head of the table in the dining room. She wore a rough, patched robe and a simple veil. Her feet were bare. As Teresa talked, the sisters around the room listened carefully. Through the teachings of this woman, each of the sisters had come to recognize the wonderful presence of God in her heart.

"O Lord Jesus," Teresa prayed, "how little do we Christians know You."

Then, she looked at her sisters and said to them, "It is no small pity, and should cause us no little shame that we do not understand ourselves, or know who we are."

Teresa of Avila spent her sixty-seven years on earth trying to know Jesus and to know herself in relation to Jesus. She knew that the Spirit of Jesus dwelt inside her and inside every person who believes in Jesus. She wrote many volumes teaching about the presence of God in the human heart and about the importance of contacting Jesus Himself in prayer—simple and personal prayer. Her most famous book is called *The Interior Castle* in which she taught how a person can grow from self-knowledge to a real awareness of the presence of Jesus. After Teresa died, her sisters found a little poem written on a bookmark in her prayer book:

Be not perplexed,
Be not afraid,
Everything passes,
God does not change.
Patience wins all things.
The one who has God lacks nothing.
Only Jesus is enough.

Teresa died in 1582. She was declared a saint in 1622. In 1970, Pope Paul VI made Teresa the first woman ever to be called a *Doctor of the Church*.

Doctor of the Church A title given to saints whose writing or preaching is helpful for Christians of all times and places. There are thirty-two doctors of the Church.

Battlefield Gospel

The First World War was an ugly war. Blood was spattered all over Europe. During the constant shellings and bombings in the battle of Treviso, Italy, everyone was scared to death. But darting from bed to bed in the field hospital was a little nun who seemed to forget the danger. She helped the wounded and the dying, she smiled, and she gave cooling drinks to the suffering. To each patient, she would offer little phrases from the Gospel and words of calming encouragement. Those who experienced the care and kindness of Sister Bertilla Boscardin felt that Jesus Himself was caring for their needs.

Annetta Boscardin was born of peasant parents. Her childhood was lonely and filled with sadness. Everyone thought that Annetta was without talent and was mentally very slow. Her friends laughed at her when she said she wanted to become a sister. People smiled again when Annetta was accepted as a Sister of Saint Dorothy and was given the name Sister Bertilla.

Her superiors did not think Sister Bertilla had much talent either, so they gave her the job of doing the laundry and scrubbing the floors. Bertilla didn't care. She spent all her free time studying and memorizing the Gospels. She would imagine scenes from the Gospels as she did her chores. She would go over and over the words of Jesus as she fingered her rosary.

In 1907, Sister Bertilla was sent to work in a children's diphtheria ward. She loved to care for the sick children and to sing them songs about Jesus. In 1915, when the war broke out in Italy, the hospital became a battlefield hospital. And Sister Bertilla spent twenty hours of every day working with all the soldiers and civilians who had been wounded. When the war moved on to another location, the general requested that Sister Bertilla come to the field hospital near Viggiu.

In 1952, when Sister Bertilla was declared one of the Blessed in heaven, many of the men and women who had experienced her care were gathered in Saint Peter's in Rome. One of them said, "When I felt the love of Sister Bertilla, I knew that Jesus lives and that Jesus loves me. Why else would He have sent Sister Bertilla to me?"

The Mystical Body

Another war was ripping through Europe. Everyone had been sure that the First World War had been the "war to end all wars." But the Second World War was worse. Hitler's armies were taking over cities and towns everywhere. In Italy, Mussolini had joined with Hitler, and people feared that soon all of Europe would be overrun and destroyed. Jews were being killed by the tens of thousands, and their bodies were being burned in huge ovens on the frontiers of Poland, Austria, and Czechoslovakia.

In the midst of this war, Pope Pius XII felt discouraged and frightened. He had been receiving reports from around the world. He could not believe the horrible things people who said they were followers of Jesus were doing. On June 29, 1943, Pope Pius issued an encyclical letter entitled *The Mystical Body*. This encyclical, one of the most beautiful ever written, was a plea with all the members of the Church to remember that they were the presence of Jesus Christ in the world. He wanted everyone to treat the members of the Body with respect and with love. The Body of Christ was suffering in the world. It was time for the followers of Jesus to wake up and realize what they were called to do and what they were called to be.

Forty Hours

The bishop of Philadelphia had just spent an hour praying before the Blessed Sacrament in the cathedral. He genuflected, made the sign of the cross, and walked thoughtfully back to his house. He had been talking to Jesus in the Eucharist. He knew how important it was for Catholics to remember the presence of Jesus in the Mass and in the Blessed Sacrament. Bishop John Nepomucene Neumann decided to revive an old custom in his diocese. He wanted every parish during the year to have a special festival in honor of Christ in the Blessed Sacrament. This festival was to be called *Forty Hours Devotion.* Around the clock for forty hours, priests, sisters, grown-ups, and children in each parish would have special Masses, visit the Blessed Sacrament, and have prayers and processions to honor Jesus.

Bishop Neumann hoped that these celebrations would remind the members of his diocese that in the Eucharist and the other sacraments, Jesus Christ was really present. He hoped that these special festivals would make it easier to believe that on the altar at Mass, the bread and wine become the Body and Blood of Jesus Christ.

John, the third bishop of Philadelphia, died in 1860. He is now Saint John Neumann—an American saint who, among other things, helped people remember the presence of the living Jesus in the Eucharistic Celebration.

Forty Hours Devotion A special tradition of honoring Jesus in the Blessed Sacrament. A parish spends almost three days in special prayers and Masses to remind the members of the parish how important and wonderful the Eucharist is in the lives of Catholics.

Questions

1. What are four ways in which Jesus is alive and present today?
2. Why is the presence of Jesus a mystery?
3. How did Saint Teresa, Saint Bertilla, Pope Pius XII, and Saint John Neumann show people the presence of Jesus?
4. In what way do you best see the presence of the living Jesus in the world today?

Activities

1. In small groups, read one of the Last Supper stories listed below. Discuss how the Apostles must have felt. Then, discuss what you might have told the Apostles about the presence of Jesus in the world today.
   a. Matthew 26:20–30
   b. Mark 14:17–26
   c. Luke 22:14–20
2. Choose one of the ways Jesus is present today and make a personal reminder for yourself. This reminder can be a bookmark, a mirror sign, or a bumper sticker. Share what you have made with your family and explain what you have done and why. Keep the reminder where you will see it frequently.

Making Jesus Present

You are a member of the Catholic Church. That is part of your personal identity. As a member of the Church, you identify with Jesus. The presence of Jesus in your life means much more than having a little "picture" of Jesus in your mind. You have a responsibility to make Jesus present, too. As a member of the Church, you can recognize Jesus, celebrate the fact that He is alive and present in the world, and you can share His presence with others.

Make a copy of the chart below. For each of the four ways Jesus is present, write one way you can recognize His presence. Then, write one way you can celebrate His presence. Finally, write one way you can share His presence with others. In the second half of the chart, write three answers to the question, "Why does Jesus make a difference to you?" Share what you have done with the class. By pooling your ideas, you can get a pretty good idea of how your class can make Jesus present in the family, neighborhood, parish, or school.

Presence of Jesus	Recognize	Celebrate	Share
1. In me			
2. In Scripture			
3. In people			
4. In the Eucharist			

Why Jesus makes a difference to me
1.
2.
3.

Review

1. What did promise Jesus His followers?

2. How can you contact Jesus in your heart?

3. How can you contact Jesus in the Gospels?

4. How can you contact Jesus in the People of God?

5. How can you contact Jesus in the sacraments?

Projects

1. The story of Lazarus and his sisters shows that Jesus recognized how painful the separation of death can be. Read the story (John 11:1–43). When you have finished, write your own answer to the question Jesus asked Martha (25–26).

2. Have a special celebration to honor people who make Jesus present for your class. Include special acknowledgments of parents, teachers, priests, parish workers, and friends.

3. Christians have traditionally remembered and thought about the words Jesus spoke while He was suffering and dying. Look up these seven "last words" listed below. How do these words help make Jesus present to you?
   a. Luke 23:34   e. John 19:28
   b. Mark 15:34   f. John 19:30
   c. John 19:26–27   g. Luke 23:46
   d. Luke 23:43

Prayer

Lord, our Lord, we sing of Your presence,
Wherever on earth we might be.
Do stay so near and mercifully by us
That Your loving hand we may see.
In all things are You deeply hidden,
In all that blossoms and unfolds.
But it is in people that You will flower,
With us in heart and in soul.

(Dutch folk tune, words by Huub Oosterhuis)

Reviewing Part Two

Summary

In this Part, you have learned several truths about your Catholic Faith.

1. Jesus is the Christ, the Son of the living God. He was sent by God the Father to bring the Father's love and to save people from sin and death.
2. Jesus Christ is truly God and truly human. He is one Person with two natures, divine and human. This union of the divine and human has been called the hypostatic union.
3. The Gospels are the Living Word of God. They are inspired by the Holy Spirit and reveal God to people.
4. The central message of the Gospels, called the kerygma, is the Good News that God has become a human being in the Incarnation and has redeemed people through His death and resurrection.
5. Christians are called not only to believe the Gospels but also to put the teachings of Jesus into action in the way they live and care for others.
6. Jesus has chosen leaders for His Church. He wants those leaders to serve others. The pope is the head of the Catholic Church, and in the pope and the bishops with the pope, the Church has the gift of infallibility — correctness in matters of faith and morals.
7. Jesus Christ is truly risen from the dead and is present in the hearts of believers, in Holy Scripture, in the Mystical Body, and in the Eucharist and the other sacraments.

Questions

1. Why is it important to know and understand the identity of Jesus?
2. What are three different titles for Jesus and what do they mean?
3. What is a mystery?
4. What are some of the kinds of writing in the Gospels?
5. What are the four ideas contained in the kerygma, or the Good News?
6. What are four of the basic rights, or human needs, mentioned by Pope John XXIII in his letter, *Peace on Earth?*
7. What kind of leaders did Jesus want for His Church?
8. What are some of the duties of the pope and the bishops?
9. What are four ways in which Jesus is alive and present in the world today?
10. What was the promise Jesus made to His friends at the Last Supper?

True or False

Circle the T if the statement is true. Circle the F if the statement is false.

1. The titles of Jesus tell that Jesus lived in the Roman Empire.   T   F
2. Jesus is only God. He just appears to be human.   T   F
3. Jesus wrote two of the Gospels Himself.   T   F
4. The Gospels contain what the believers thought was most important about Jesus.   T   F
5. There are no facts known about Jesus at all.   T   F
6. Loving, believing, and hoping are some of the skills learned from studying the Gospels.   T   F

7. Christians are supposed to put the words of the
   Gospels into action.   T   F
8. The bishop of Rome became important because Rome
   was the largest city in the world.   T   F
9. The pope and the bishops help people stay faithful to
   the truth.   T   F
10. Jesus is really present in the Eucharist.   T   F

Matching

Match the item in column B which best identifies each
person in column A.

A	B
1. ___ Mark	a. His Gospel showed Jesus as the Word of God.
2. ___ John	
3. ___ Louise de Marillac	b. She showed the Gospel in her actions toward the sick and wounded.
4. ___ Teresa of Avila	
5. ___ Pope John XXIII	c. She showed that Jesus is present in the hearts of believers.
6. ___ Saint Bertilla	
7. ___ Saint John Neumann	d. He urged people to have devotion to Jesus present in the Blessed Sacrament.
	e. She helped start the Daughters of Charity.
	f. He wrote *Peace on Earth*.
	g. His Gospel was written for Roman Christians.

Vocabulary

Use the following terms in a sentence.

Church	synoptic
encyclical	inspiration
theologians	religious vows
synod	Doctor of the Church

Celebration

Plan a special prayer service or a class Mass to celebrate Jesus, His life, His death, and His resurrection. Use prayers, readings, and ideas from this Part of the book. Set aside a special time for the Mass or service. Remember, your celebration should show who Jesus is, the basic Good News Jesus gave, the importance of putting the Gospels into action, the leadership of service in the Church, and the presence of Jesus today. Pages 284–285 of your Handbook will help you with your plans. Be sure to include music and actions.

On one occasion a lawyer stood up to pose
Jesus this problem: "Teacher, what must I do to
inherit everlasting life?"
Jesus answered him: "What is written in the
law? How do you read it?"
The lawyer replied:
"You shall love the Lord your God
with all your heart,
with all your soul,
with all your strength,
and with all your mind;
and your neighbor as yourself."
Jesus said, "You have answered correctly. Do
this and you shall live."

(Luke 10:25–28)

PART THREE

Signs of a New Covenant

13

A House Built on Rock

In This Chapter

You will see how Jesus challenges you to take responsibility for your own actions.

You will discover your own ability to be responsible.

You will learn that growing in responsibility requires a good foundation.

Planning for the Future

One of the most embarrassing times can be the visit of an adult relative or friend of the family whom you haven't seen for a while. Often, you have to listen to remarks like "My, how big you're getting!" or "You're getting to be quite a young lady (or gentleman)." Even though those remarks sound funny or embarrassing, they point to a very important fact—you are growing and changing.

You are not an adult. You do not do the things adults do. But then again, you are no longer a child either. You are branching out, learning new things, acting more and more on your own. You may even be making plans for your future. You may have some idea of what you would like to be and do during your life.

Take this opportunity to make some plans—just as an exercise. Choose one of the five future goals listed at the end of this section. For a few moments,

imagine what it would be like to have reached this goal. Imagine what you would be doing, how you would act, and how others would treat you.

After you have spent a few moments with those imaginings, make a list of four steps you would have to take to reach the goal you have chosen. Two of the steps should be about *attitudes* you would have to have. And the other two steps should be about *skills* you would have to develop. When you have finished, discuss what you have written with the class.

1. I am a world-class figure skater.
2. I am a university professor of social studies.
3. I am a world-renowned movie star.
4. I am a famous artist (painter, sculptor, or musician).
5. I am a brother, sister, or priest.

Attitudes and skills An attitude is the way people have of looking at things. A skill is the habitual way people have of acting. Christian attitudes and skills give people a sense of their identity as members of God's People.

Goal	Attitudes	Skills
	1.	1.
	2.	2.

Questions

1. What were your reasons for choosing the goal you chose?
2. Which kinds of plans do you consider most important—attitudes or skills? Explain your answer.
3. What are some of your real future plans? What attitudes and skills are you developing right now to help you reach those goals?

Activities

1. Continue the planning exercise by making a list of three very possible and very realistic personal goals you have. Then, try to discover what attitudes and skills you would need to develop for those goals. This time, instead of answering the question, "What would I like to *be and do?*" answer the question, "What *kind of person* do I want to be?"
2. Spend an hour or two watching television with the family. Keep an "attitude and skills log" on one of the characters in the show you are watching. From what you observe, what kind of person is the character?

Children of the Covenant

hatever you want to do or whatever you want to be is going to take planning and practice. You are going to have to make choices. You are going to have to develop a way of acting and behaving. A person's way of acting or behaving is sometimes called a person's *ethics*, or morality. As you grow and develop as a person, you have to develop a way of making choices and of acting. You have to develop certain attitudes toward life, and you have to develop certain skills, too.

Ethics The study of behavior which shows the difference between right and wrong. Christian ethics is sometimes called morality.

The Sermon on the Mount

Imagine that you are seated in a crowd on a grassy hillside. You are listening to a teacher who has come to tell about a new way to live. The speaker is telling about a God and Father who loves His children and who wants His children to be happy. Then, the speaker begins to tell about the attitudes and skills that the loving God expects of His children.

Two thousand years ago, Jesus stood on a hillside in Israel and spoke to the people about a covenant with God the Father—a covenant of love and goodness. He wanted His hearers to grow and to develop in the attitudes and skills it takes to live up to their part of that covenant.

"How blest are the poor in spirit: the reign of God is theirs. . . . Blest are the peacemakers; they shall be called children of God.

"You are the salt of the earth. But what if salt goes flat? Then, it is good for nothing. You are the light of the world. A city set on a hill cannot be hidden. In the same way, your light must shine before others so that they may see goodness in your acts and give praise to your heavenly Father.

"You have heard the commandment, 'You shall not commit murder.' What I say to you is: everyone who grows angry shall be liable to judgment. Anyone who uses abusive language toward others shall be answerable, too. You have heard the commandment, 'You shall love your country but hate your enemies.' My command to you is: love your enemies, pray for those who do you harm."

(Matthew 5:3, 9, 13–16, 21–22, 43–44)

Responsibility and Conscience

You are a member of the Church. God's People are people who try to act, to think, and to behave like faithful children of the covenant. They try to take the message of Jesus and turn that message into a way of living. To say "I am a Christian" means "I act like a Christian, and I have Christian attitudes."

Part of growing up is learning to take *responsibility* for one's actions. But responsibility does not happen automatically. Responsibility is a very important skill you can learn. When the skill is

Responsibility Being answerable for one's thoughts, words, and actions. People who try to follow the laws of God and the Church are showing Christian responsibility.

mastered, it is much easier to act like a follower of Jesus. On that same hillside, Jesus taught people about responsibility.

"Anyone who hears My words and puts them into practice is like the wise one who built a house on rock. When the rainy season set in, the torrents came and the winds blew and beat on the house. It did not collapse; it had been solidly set on rock. Anyone who hears My words but does not put them into practice is like the foolish one who built a house on sandy ground. The rains fell, the torrents came, the winds blew and beat against the house. It collapsed under all this and was completely ruined."

(Matthew 7:24–27)

Learning what is right and wrong, developing good Christian attitudes, and mastering Christian skills are the ways to build your house on rock. Throughout this Part of the book, you will be learning more of these actions, attitudes, and skills—signs that you are responding to the covenant of love which Jesus taught about.

Inside you, you have a great help to building your house on rock. This tool is called your conscience. Your conscience is a judgment you make about whether something is right or wrong. Part of building your house on rock is using your conscience and training your judgment to know what is right and to choose what is right.

Mother and Son

Monica was very worried about her son. He was a runaway. He laughed at some of the rules and regulations of the Church. He often gambled. He drank too much wine. He had quite a bad reputation. Monica prayed for her son. She knew that down deep, he really wanted much more out of life than what he was getting. Somehow, Monica knew that her son would stop building his house on sand and start building it on rock. One day, when Monica's son was in the city of Milan, Italy, he heard a famous preacher telling about Christ's Sermon on the Mount. Monica's son was touched to the heart. He went to the preacher and said that he wanted to change and to grow. He said that he was tired of living the way he had been living and wanted to seek the truth.

Monica was very happy when she heard the news. She had never given up praying for her son. The young man who had been building his house on sand became one of the greatest teachers the Catholic Church has ever known. Monica's son became the great Saint Augustine of Hippo. He is even called a Father and Doctor of the Church. In one of his writings, Augustine explained in a prayer why he stopped building his house on sand and started building it on the rock of Jesus Christ. "You have made us for Yourself, O Lord," Augustine prayed, "and our hearts are restless until they rest in You."

Questions

1. What does it mean to build your house on rock?
2. What is your conscience? How does it help you show that you are a child of God's covenant?
3. What is one Christian action which you do regularly? What is one Christian attitude you have? What is one Christian skill you have developed?
4. In your words, what does being responsible mean?

Activities

1. In each of the passages listed below, God is described as a rock. In small groups, read three of the passages and discuss what each means. How can you use the passages as prayers to help you "build on rock"?
   a. Psalm 18:1–20
   b. Psalm 28:1, 8–9
   c. Psalm 42:7–12
   d. Psalm 62:1–9
   e. Psalm 89:21–28
   f. 2 Samuel 22:2–4
2. Share the story of Saint Monica and Saint Augustine with your family. Then, discuss three ways the members of your family can help one another build on rock. Share what you have decided with the class.

Forming
Your Conscience

Part of building your house on rock is making sure that your conscience is in good working order—that it can choose between what is right and what is wrong. The words and teachings of Jesus are the best helps to forming a good conscience.

Using the chart below as a guide, study the Sermon on the Mount from the Gospel of Saint Matthew. For each of the moral subjects mentioned, read the part of the sermon listed. Then, describe what you think is an important Christian attitude toward the subject and what skills a Christian would need to be responsible and in good conscience about the subject. Discuss what you have written in class. Make a master list of attitudes and skills.

Subject	Attitudes	Skills
1. Keeping the law (5:17–21)		
2. Conflict (5:22–26)		
3. Purity (5:27–32)		
4. Language (5:33–37)		
5. Relationships (5:38–48, 7:12–14)		
6. Caring (6:1–4)		
7. Prayer and fasting (6:5–18, 7:7–11)		
8. Money (6:19–34)		
9. Judging others (7:1–6)		

Review

Label each of the following sentences to show whether it is an attitude or a skill. Use the letter *S* for a skill and the letter *A* for an attitude.

1. ___ Blest are the singled-hearted for they shall see God.

2. ___ Turn the other cheek.

3. ___ Pray to your Father in your room.

4. ___ Treat others the way you want them to treat you.

5. ___ Be glad because your reward is great in heaven.

6. ___ Forgive one another from the heart.

7. ___ Let your light shine before others, so they can see the good you do.

Projects

1. In a journal or in a private notebook, record one example of each of the nine subjects mentioned in the chart in this section. Make the examples real. Then, in your own words, write what your attitude is toward each example.

2. Have a brief prayer service using the Beatitudes (Matthew 5:3–12). Page 288 of your Handbook will help you put the service together. During the service, talk about how the attitudes found in the Beatitudes can help you build your house on rock.

3. Make a bulletin-board reminder for your home which tells of the importance of building your house on rock. Explain the reminder to your family. Put it somewhere in your home where you will see it every day.

Prayer

Happy are people who are without blame,
   who walk in the law of the Lord.
Happy are the ones who observe His rules,
   who seek Him with all their hearts,
   and do no wrong but walk in His ways.

(Psalm 119:1–3)

14

A Struggle to Respond

In This Chapter

You will explore reasons why people fail to follow the Way of Jesus.

You will review the meaning of sin.

You will discover helps for you to follow the new covenant.

Love Means Action

gnatius was bored. He was a soldier, not an invalid. He had been in this room for a month. The wounds he had received in battle were beginning to heal, but it would be a few more weeks before he could even walk. He wanted at least to be back at Loyola Castle in the beautiful Basque countryside.

Three books were piled on Ignatius's bed stand. For the hundredth time, Ignatius pulled them onto the bed. "Religious books," he muttered. "All I have to read are religious books. Who do they think I am, a monk? I am a soldier. I do what I please, and I fight for glory and the sheer pleasure of it. What would I want with these books of holy sayings?"

But boredom won. Ignatius began by reading the book of the Gospels. He read it carefully and with interest. When he got to the end of Saint John's Gospel, he let the book slip to the blanket. "I have heard those words since I was a boy, 'Love one another as I have loved you,'" Ignatius spoke aloud to himself. "But they are impossible. There is too much selfishness in people, too much greed, too much lust, too much pride, and too much hate. No one can defeat those enemies, except perhaps the sword. That kind of love just won't work!"

Two other books stared up at Ignatius from the bedclothes, a life of Saint Dominic and a life of Saint Francis. Through the next days and weeks, Ignatius read the books over and over again. The Gospels told him about a way of living based on truth, faith, caring, and love. The stories of the two saints told him that the enemies—selfishness, greed, pride, and hate—could be beaten.

In the year 1552, Ignatius Loyola knelt in the great abbey church of Montserrat. Before the image of the Blessed Mother, Ignatius gave up his soldier's

sword. But Ignatius was not giving up battle. He was instead forming a new army to fight a new battle. Now, Ignatius and his followers were going to arm themselves with truth and with love. They were going to fight for the Gospels. They were going to use prayer, study, teaching, preaching, and loyalty to the People of God. These tools would help people follow Jesus.

Ignatius called his new army the Company of Jesus. Today, that group is called the Society of Jesus—the Jesuits. The Spanish soldier became a great saint because he showed that with the help of God, people could win over selfishness. They could follow the love commandment of Jesus. They could live and do all "for the greater glory of God."

Questions

1. What was Ignatius's attitude toward religion?
2. How did that attitude change?
3. Why did Ignatius look at the commandment of Jesus like a struggle or battle?
4. Can you remember a time when you had to struggle to do what was right? Describe what happened. How did you feel? How did you act?

Activities

1. Choose two teams for a debate. One side will argue that it is impossible to follow the love commandment of Jesus in the world today. The other side will argue that not only is it possible but also most necessary. Begin the debate by reading aloud John 13:31–35, 14:14–21. The class can then summarize and discuss the points the debaters have brought out.

2. As homework, find one story in the newspaper or on the television news that shows someone struggling to do what is right. Report on the story in class.

Sin Is Real

God did not create robots. Jesus did not come to teach and save computers by putting a good and loving program into a series of microprocessors. God made people free. Jesus came to invite people into God's kingdom of love, justice, and peace. People are free to respond.

The Adam and Eve story in the Bible shows how when people are free to choose, they can choose to do what is wrong. The sin of the first human beings is called *original sin.* That same term describes what every free human person has felt—the real struggle to do what is right.

When a person freely chooses to do something he or she knows is morally wrong, that person commits a sin. Always choosing what you know is right is not easy. It is not easy because, inside your heart, there is a pull away from what is good and right. There are excuses you can make to yourself for choosing what is wrong.

Original sin The first sin, the sin of Adam and Eve. Original sin describes the pull everyone feels toward doing what is wrong.

A Tug-of-War

Saint Paul, when he was teaching people about following Jesus, talked about a tug-of-war between the *flesh* and the *spirit.* Saint Paul did not mean that you are neatly divided into two parts—good spirit and bad body. What Paul was describing was the tendency in people to be selfish and uncaring, the flesh. Jesus, on the other hand, invites His friends to be open, caring, and unselfish, the spirit. Saint Paul wrote, "The flesh wars against the spirit, and the spirit against the flesh; the two are directly opposed" *(Galatians 5:17).*

On the side of the flesh, Saint Paul lined up actions and attitudes which are against everything

Flesh and spirit In the Bible, the term *flesh* sometimes refers to selfishness, and the term *spirit* refers to unselfishness.

Jesus taught. Some of these are impurity, worshiping idols, superstition, hostility, bickering, jealousy, angry outbursts, rivalries, factions, envy, drunkenness, and overeating. On the spirit side, Saint Paul lined up love, joy, peace, patient endurance, kindness, generosity, faith, gentleness, and modesty.

The flesh team is called the *vices*. The spirit team is called the *virtues*. The stage is set for the tug-of-war. You can picture it just like a tug-of-war on field day at school or at a company picnic. You can feel it inside yourself when you have a choice to make. You forgot to do your homework. As your teacher is collecting the papers, you feel the vice team and the virtue team fighting it out inside. It would be very easy to make up a lie about your homework. It would be hard to face the teacher and just admit that you forgot to do it. When the teacher reaches your desk, you look him in the eye and say, "I am very sorry, but I forgot to do my homework." The virtues win!

Down through the years, the Church has really made up two official teams for the tug-of-war. The first of these teams is called the seven capital sins— bad habits of acting which make it difficult for a follower of Jesus to choose what is right. The second team is called the seven capital virtues—good habits of acting which make it easier to choose what is right. The little chart below will help you line up these two teams to see how the tug-of-war takes place.

Vices and virtues Vices are bad habits of acting, and virtues are good habits of acting. Avoiding vices and practicing virtue make people stronger in their faith.

TUG-OF-WAR

Seven Capital Sins	Seven Capital Virtues
1. Pride	1. Humility
2. Covetousness	2. Generosity
3. Lust	3. Chastity
4. Anger	4. Gentleness
5. Gluttony	5. Temperance
6. Envy	6. Friendship
7. Laziness	7. Diligence

As you can see, the more a person works on coaching and developing the virtues team, the more likely the good side is going to win the tug-of-war. You can also see that you are responsible for the tug-of-war. The desire to do what is right, to follow Jesus, and to have Christian attitudes, actions, and skills must be in your heart. Family, friends, priests, sisters, and others can help you, but what goes on in your heart is most important. You have to *want* to do what is right.

Making Excuses

As if the tug-of-war were not enough, free people have the ability to make excuses for acting or not acting, for choosing to do wrong rather than to do right. Excuses are designed to help a person wriggle out of responsibility for his or her actions and attitudes. Excuses are a way to say, "Don't blame me."

Jesus told a story about a rich landowner who was giving a great dinner party. He sent out many invitations. When the day of the party arrived, the landowner sent out servants to bring in the invited guests. The guests started to make excuses for not coming. One said that he had just bought land and was on his way to inspect it. He could not make it to the party. Another had just bought oxen and wanted to try them. So, he could not make it. Another had just gotten married. So, he would not be coming either. You can read the whole story in Luke 14:16–24.

Behind the words of common excuses plays quite a different tune:

1. This is too hard for me! (I am too lazy. I want the easy way out.)
2. This is not my job. Someone else should be responsible. (I would like to push my responsibility off on someone else.)
3. I didn't know what to do. (I did not make the effort to learn the rules, to develop the attitudes, or to practice the skills.)
4. Everyone does it. (I do not have the courage to do what I know is right.)
5. I am only human. (I do not expect very much of myself. I am willing to settle for less than the best.)

Feed the Hungry: An Example

When Jesus was teaching about love, He said to the Apostles, "I was hungry and you gave me food.... Whatever you did to these little ones, you did for Me." Throughout the history of the Church, the followers of Jesus have realized that feeding people in need is part of Christian love in action.

Today, the world is a pretty hungry place. Almost two-thirds of the world's people go to bed with a hungry feeling in the pit of the stomach. Almost one-third of the world's people are actually suffering from malnourishment or even starvation.

For the followers of Jesus, these facts mean something for the choices they have to make. They realize that what they choose to do or not do about the use of food, energy, and natural resources can have an effect on the world. So, the followers of Jesus want to know what their responsibilities are. They want to know what they can and ought to do. Next, they want to see how the tug-of-war inside them will affect the problem of hunger. What is pulling them away from doing the right thing to make the world a less hungry place?

The followers of Jesus want to examine the excuses they might offer for not doing anything to help the hungry or to use food, energy, and natural resources correctly. They also want to have a personal plan of action. They want to do what is possible to help the hungry. Finally, they want to help one another struggle to give food to the hungry.

This little process of choosing can be used for any moral choice, from using drugs or alcohol to telling the truth. It is a struggle to respond to Jesus and His commandment of love. But to succeed in the struggle to do what is right, it is very important to have a good plan of action.

Questions

1. Why is Christian morality described as a tug-of-war?

2. Why do people make excuses for acting or not acting according to what they know is right?

3. What are two common excuses for making wrong choices? What is behind those excuses?

4. How have you experienced the struggle to make a right choice? Describe how you felt and acted.

Activities

1. Choose one of the passages listed below. Read the passage. When you have finished, write your own definition of a virtue and of a vice. Share what you have written with the rest of the class.
   a. Ephesians 4:32—5:7
   b. Colossians 3:12–17
   c. Ephesians 4:25–31
   d. Colossians 3:5–10

2. Have a classroom tug-of-war between the vices and the virtues. Choose sides. Then, someone can read situations out of the daily newspaper that call for Christian choice or action. The vices can argue for their side, and the virtues for theirs to determine what action should be taken. The teacher may wish to referee the tug-of-war, or one of the students can referee.

Plan of Action

I t is not enough to say that you believe in Jesus Christ and in His new covenant of love. You have to put that love to work in the way you think and act. As you have learned, there is a struggle going on between good and evil—love and selfishness. Take this opportunity to practice a plan of action. Listed below are three examples of the kind of response Jesus taught His followers. Read each of the examples. Then, using the chart as a guide, (1) describe your responsibility, (2) describe what tug-of-war could take place in you, (3) give any excuses you might make, (4) describe something you can do to put the new covenant into action, and (5) describe how you can help one another make the right choice. Discuss what you have done in class.

Strategy	Luke 6:27–28	Mark 11:24–25	John 14:20–21
Responsibility			
Tug-of-War			
Excuses			
Action			
Help			

Review

Circle the T if the statement is true. Circle the F if the statement is false.

1. Saint Ignatius did not see any real struggle in living up to the Gospel.   T   F

2. Saint Paul described trying to make good moral choices as a war between flesh and spirit.   T   F

3. Virtues are good habits which make it easier to choose what is right.   T   F

4. Christians only have responsibility for not doing anything wrong.   T   F

5. It is important to have a personal plan of action for putting Jesus' love commandment into action.   T   F

Projects

1. Take the strategy given in this chapter and put the five steps in the form of questions you can ask yourself when you have to make a moral choice. Use the five questions for a day. At the end of the day, describe in writing what happened. You may want to discuss what happened with friends or in class.

2. Prayer is a very important part of doing what is right. Write a short prayer, in your own words, that you might use as a night prayer for a week. The prayer should ask Jesus for help in putting His love commandment into action. Pages 284–285 of your Handbook will help you write this prayer.

Prayer

Lord, this solemn prayer comes from deep desire.
May my life be as pure as candle fire.
Let my every breath dispel the world's gloom.
Let my spirit be so bright that darkness meets its doom.
May my life be devoted to serving the needy
And to loving a sorrowful, suffering humanity.
Lead me away from the path of temptation.
O Lord, let truth and good be my destination.

(From a Pakistani children's prayer)

15

Love Is Patient

In This Chapter

You will discover that patience is an important virtue for Christians.

You will learn the qualities of patient love.

You will see how you can develop these qualities by following Jesus and the example of others.

The Quick-Fix

oday, people want results, and they want them now! The word *fast* is attached to almost everything people need or do. Fast food, fast relief, fast answers, quick cash, instant success, and many more phrases like that sprinkle through daily conversation. Watch any hour of television, and you will see ads for ways of becoming wonderful all at once. Beer, wine, pizza, doughnuts, breakfast cereal, and even spaghetti sauce can make you feel happier immediately.

Purchasing a new car can change your self-image. Perfume or shampoo can make you immediately attractive. Knowing and having the newest record or tape shows how up-to-date you are. Video games can make you forget your troubles in a barrage of beeps and pongs.

You probably have a very serious desire to be grown up, to do what you want to do, to go where you want to go. You may even get very impatient with the time it is taking you to mature. It would not be surprising if you were looking for the "quick-fix"—instant answers to the feelings and wishes you have.

Listed below are some statements which express very common feelings. Read each statement carefully. For each statement, write one quick-fix—one easy answer. Then, write one answer that would take more time to work out but which just might be more permanent.

1. "I don't feel like anybody cares for me."
2. "Sometimes, I feel very, very lonely."
3. "My parents just don't understand me anymore."
4. "I feel there is just nothing to do around here."
5. "I really get scared of the future sometimes."
6. "Once in a while, I don't like myself very much."
7. "School is so hard that I just feel like quitting."
8. "I never get invited anywhere; what's wrong with me?"

Questions

1. Why do advertisers try so hard to sell the quick-fix?
2. Why do you think quick-and-easy answers to problems are so appealing?
3. Do you ever feel impatient? What makes you impatient? How do you act when you are being impatient?

Activities

1. Discuss three examples of quick-fixes that you have seen or heard in the last twenty-four hours. What do they promise? Why are they so appealing?
2. Write a radio or television ad for patience. Use some of the language and imagery of advertisements for quick-fixes. Share what you have done in class.

God's Time

The desire for instant answers is not new. The Scripture tells the story of Job, who suffered all kinds of misfortunes and trials. Job lost everything—family, lands, herds, money. Three of Job's friends tried to tell Job to blame God. But Job was patient. He understood that the universe was not running on his time but on God's.

The Apostles were often impatient. They were always asking Jesus when He would restore the kingdom of Israel. They wanted Jesus to get rid of His enemies at once. They were anxious to receive the praise and recognition they thought they would get for being friends with someone so powerful.

The message of Jesus was clear. Love is patient. Impatience can lead to wrong choices—even sin. To show His friends what He meant, Jesus told a little story:

"A landowner had a fig tree growing in his vineyard, and he came out looking for fruit on it but did not find any. He said to the vinedresser, 'Look here! For three years now, I have come in search of fruit on this fig tree and found none. Cut it down. Why should it clutter up the ground?' In answer, the vinedresser said, 'Sir, leave it another year while I hoe around it and fertilize it. Then, perhaps, it will bear fruit. If not, it shall be cut down.'"

(Luke 13:6–9)

People who forget that love is patient are always finding ways to cut down fig trees. Some people use drugs to cut down their fig trees. They want to feel better. They want to feel grown up. They want to escape from the pressures of school. Or, they want to make points with friends. They do not see far enough ahead to know the danger of drugs. They do not have time to see what could happen to their bodies and their emotions. So, they choose drugs, and instead of finding love, they face sickness, prison, and even death.

Some people use alcohol to cut down their fig trees. They think that drinking can make them feel happier all at once. They want to look and to act sophisticated. They forget that alcohol *addiction* is a terrible and often fatal disease. The younger the body subjected to alcohol, the more serious the consequences.

Drugs, alcohol, food, smoking, and bad health habits can all be ways of fig-tree forestry. You look at yourself. You do not like what you see. So, you want to get rid of what you see as a great big fruit-less fig tree. But that is not the way of God's king-dom and the convenant love of Jesus.

Addiction The mental or physical need for some substance. A person who needs drugs or alcohol is said to suffer from drug or alcohol addiction.

Qualities of Patient Love

Patient love is a very important skill for the fol-lowers of Jesus. By patient love, Christians bring the love of Jesus to the ones who need it most. By patient love, Christians are willing to stick to the task of learning about Jesus and His message, put-ting that message in their hearts, and sharing that message by the way they act. But it is also very important to recognize the qualities of patient love. If you can see the signs of patient love in yourself, then you know you are growing. If the signs are missing, you may need some help to develop them.

1. *A sense of self-worth.* It is most important that you know that you are good, special, valuable, and loved. That is the beginning of patient love. If you feel worthless to yourself, it is going to be very difficult to share yourself with others. People who feel worthless can be very easily tempted by the quick-fix.
2. *Self-discipline.* Patient love knows the importance of hard work to reach a goal, to grow, and to help others. A good sense of self-discipline means that a person can see the value of going step-by-

step and not rushing. Patient love is willing to give up small pleasures because it is working for a bigger goal.

3. *Overcoming obstacles.* Patient love knows that things are going to go wrong. There are going to be potholes in the road. There are going to be mistakes. But patient love is always ready to start over and to learn from mistakes. Patient love is sure that no mistake is fatal.

4. *Investing time.* You know that you have patient love if you are willing to spend time for others. Roller-coaster rides last only a couple of minutes, but life's journey is lived day in, day out. You can tell how much you value a person or a job or a hobby by the amount of time you are willing to invest.

These four qualities can be learned. Just like the vinedressser in the story Jesus told, you can hoe around your fig tree with these qualities. Then, your patient love can help you make good choices— choices which help you grow and give of yourself to others.

The Holy Alcoholic

In Glasnevin Cemetery in Dublin, Ireland, there is a simple grave. The grave has been there since 1925, but for many years, there was no gravestone. Even now, there is only a fairly simple stone. Every day, somebody can be found kneeling in prayer before the grave. The grave, which for years was know simply as plot SK 319½, bears this simple inscription:

SACRED TO THE MEMORY
OF
MATT TALBOT
WHO DIED
7TH JUNE 1925 AGED 68
THIS MONUMENT
HAS BEEN ERECTED BY
THE MEMBERS OF THE SODALITY
OF OUR LADY IMMACULATE
SAINT FRANCIS XAVIER'S CHURCH
UPPER GARDINER STREET
OF WHICH HE WAS
A FERVENT MEMBER FOR 40 YEARS

What the marker does not say is that for his whole life, Matt Talbot struggled with a terrible disease—alcoholism. In his youth, Matt started drinking. His drinking almost destroyed his family. Matt himself almost died. He ended up in the gutter. But somebody reached out to Matt with the message of God's love.

When Matt was drinking, he did not think much of himself. But slowly, he began to realize just how much God loved him. And Matt began to return that love. It took every ounce of faith and strength Matt could muster to keep him from the bottle, and it did not happen all at once. Matt had to invest the rest of his life overcoming many, many obstacles.

Matt became active in the parish church. He helped, he cared, and he spent time with people who needed him. Matt also knew how much he needed God's help. So, Matt spent much time praying before the Blessed Sacrament.

Now, people stopping by Matt's grave are asking Matt for a sip of his patient love: "Matt, put in a word for my husband. He still doesn't have a job," prays a young wife. "Matt, ask God to help me get off drugs," prays a Dublin teenager. People ask Matt for help because they see by looking at Matt a real lesson for followers of Jesus—"Love is patient."

Questions

1. Why is patience so important for a person?
2. What are the four qualities of patient love?
3. What is the lesson of the story of the fig tree?
4. Which of the four qualities of patient love is the hardest for you? Why?

Activities

1. Read 1 Corinthians 13:1–13. When you have finished, complete the following sentence in your own words: "Love is . . ." Discuss what you have written.

2. Make a poster or bulletin-board display on "caring for the fig tree." On the display, put examples of patient love and examples of how people can cut down their fig trees.

Practicing Patience

While learning about patient love from the words of Jesus or the actions of people like Matt Talbot is important, it is not enough. To put the new covenant to work in your life, you have to start practicing patient love. You have to begin developing this very special Christian skill.

Using the chart below as a guide, find the signs of patient love in your actions, and make plans for growing in patient love. First, pick one example of each of the qualities as you show that quality now. Describe how you show that quality. Then, describe one way in which you can improve in that quality. Finally, describe one way you can use that quality to reach out to someone in need.

Quality	How I Show It	Improvement	Reach Out
Self-worth			
Discipline			
Overcoming obstacles			
Investing time			

Review

1. List three examples of a quick-fix.

2. In your own words, describe the lesson of the parable of the fig tree.

3. Give one example for each of the qualities of patient love.

4. In one sentence, what is the lesson of Matt Talbot's life?

Projects

1. Many people look for a quick-fix from feelings of boredom. Make a catalog of things to do in your neighborhood. You might entitle the booklet "What to Do When There Is Nothing to Do." Fill the catalog with community resources, sporting events and activities, cultural activities, volunteer opportunities, and the like. Include bus schedules and other transportation information. Reproduce this catalog and share it with other classes, family members, and friends.

2. Alcohol abuse and drug addiction are real enemies of patient love. Appoint a committee to find out more about the problem and the solutions that are available in your community. Part of the project could be the formulation of a class strategy to prevent drug and alcohol abuse in the class. Try to include in your strategy the attitudes you can develop toward people who have these problems.

Prayer

My heart is patient, O God; my heart is patient.
I will sing and chant Your praise.
I will awake at dawn.
I will give You thanks among all the people.
For Your kindness towers to the heavens,
   and Your faithfulness to the skies.
Be praised, O Father, for Your never ending love.

(Adapted from Psalm 108)

16

Love Is Kind

In This Chapter

You will discover that kindness and peacefulness are signs of the new covenant of love.

You will learn that violence is one of the greatest enemies of Christian kindness.

You will practice ways of bringing peace and kindness to others.

Remember Sister Maura

 he long Thanksgiving weekend was coming to an end. The group of sisters and priests who had been meeting at the *casa cural,* or parish rectory, in Diriamba, Nicaragua, were just finishing the celebration of Mass. All of the men and women were returning to their own parishes and missions throughout Central America. They had spent the last five days praying and planning how they could show God's love to the people of Panama, Nicaragua, and El Salvador.

The main celebrant of the Mass asked anyone who wished, to pray aloud in thanksgiving. After a moment, Sister Maura Clarke said a prayer, "Even though I am somewhat fearful of the difficult days ahead for our people of El Salvador, I feel convinced, dear Lord, that You want me there—that You will give me the light and strength I need." At six o'clock the next morning, Sister Maura and her friend, Sister Ita Ford, got on a small plane to return to their work in Chalatenango, El Salvador.

Sister Maura had become a Maryknoll Sister in 1950. From 1959 to 1976, she had lived and worked in Nicaragua—most of the time in a little mining town called Siuna. There, she had taught catechism, helped the sick, visited people in their homes, and led prayers for the people in outlying districts. Everyone who ever met Sister Maura remembered her kind smile and her eagerness to help.

For four years, Sister Maura had returned to the United States. She spent her time studying and teaching about the world's needs and how the followers of Jesus could lovingly respond to those needs. After this time, Sister Maura prayed about what she should do next. She felt that Nicaragua needed her, so she decided to return. In a letter she wrote to friends in Nicaragua, Sister Maura talked about her return. She wrote, "My dream is that, with each of you, in Jesus our source of hope and joy, I may continue to give myself to bring about the new kingdom of love, justice, and peace."

After just a few months back in Nicaragua, Sister Maura was asked to move to El Salvador. She was needed there. There was a civil war going on, and she could be a great help to the poor people in the rural areas. Sister Maura went without questioning. With Sister Ita, she helped search out the missing. She prayed with the families of prisoners. She helped bury the dead. Every day she worked with the poor people who were so afraid of the violence that went on around them.

Now, on December 2, 1980, Sister Maura and Sister Ita were landing in El Salvador. They were excited and happy about getting back to their people and their work. They were met at the airport by two friends, Sister Dorothy Kazel and Jean Donovan, a lay missionary. The two were going to drive Sister Maura and Sister Ita back to Chalatenango. A few hours later, probably about ten o'clock, shots were heard by the people in the area. The bullets brutally put an end to the lives of Sister Maura, Sister Ita, Sister Dorothy, and Jean Donovan.

These brave women wanted to serve others. They wanted to do their part to be kind and loving. They took some very big chances to show love to others. Their kindness proved to be so dangerous that they were killed. Once, someone had asked Sister Maura what her goal in life was. She answered with a twinkle in her eye, "To love and to serve Jesus wherever I find Him."

Questions

1. What was the basic attitude Sister Maura showed in her life and work?
2. What Christian skills did Sister Maura and her friends have?
3. What is your personal reaction to the life and death of Sister Maura and her friends?

Activities

1. Choose one of the Scripture stories listed below. Read the story aloud in a small group. Then, discuss how love was being shared in the story and what obstacles there were to that love.
   a. Matthew 26:47–56
   b. Acts 5:17–42
   c. Acts 6:8—7:1–2, 54–60
   d. Acts 16:20–40
2. List three places in your community where love is needed but where there might be some danger to bring love. Share your lists in class.

Swords into Plowshares

John was very, very old. He could not walk on his own anymore. He had to be carried from place to place. Every Sunday, John's students would carry him to the house where the Christians were gathering for the Eucharistic Meal. Everyone wanted to hear what John had to say because he was the last living Apostle. He was the last one who had been with Jesus.

Very often, the old man would repeat himself, but nobody cared. Whenever John spoke, the truth of his words would burn in their hearts. One Sunday morning, after the believers had shared prayers and songs, they all looked at John. "Tell us, Father John," someone requested, "what is the message of Jesus?"

There was fire in the old man's eyes as he wiped his lips with his frail, almost transparent hand. He gave the believers one of his oldest sermons as if it were the very first time he had ever said the words.

"This, remember, is the message
   you heard from the beginning:
   we should love one another.
We should not follow the example of Cain
   who belonged to the evil one
   and killed his brother.
Why did he kill him?
Because his own deeds were wicked
   while his brother's were just.
No need, then, brothers and sisters, to be surprised
   if the world hates you.
That we have passed from death to life we know
   because we love one another.
The one who does not love is among
   the living dead.
People who hate are murderers,
   and you know that eternal life
   abides in no murderer's heart.

The way we came to understand love
    was that Jesus laid down His life for us;
    we too must lay down our lives for others.
I ask you, how can God's love survive in a
    person who has enough of this world's goods
    yet closes his or her heart to a brother or sister
    when there is need there?
Little children,
    let us love in deed and in truth
    and not merely talk about it.
This is our way of knowing we are committed to
    the truth
    and are at peace before God."

(1 John 3:11–19)

Everyone was silent. They knew the truth of what he was saying. They remembered that the prophet Isaiah had told the people of Israel how they could recognize the kingdom of God when the Messiah came. The followers of the Messiah would bring love and peace. They would "beat their swords into plowshares and their spears into pruning hooks; one nation shall not raise the sword against another, nor shall they train for war again." John blessed the believers and signaled it was time to break bread.

The Violence Solution

The kind of love Jesus taught has enemies. All the enemies of love could be summed up in one word—violence. Violence is a symptom that something is wrong. If you wake up some morning with a scratchy throat, a headache, aches and pains, and an upset stomach, you know pretty well that you have the flu. You know because you recognize the symptoms.

When you read the paper and see stories of violence—murder, rape, assassination, street fighting, war—you know that something is wrong. There is sickness in each of the situations described. It is safe to say that wherever there is violence, something has gone wrong.

There are many different kinds of violence. Quarreling is a form of violence. So is name-calling or strong language. Fighting is violence whether that fighting is on the playground over who is safe on first base or in the Middle East over who can live on the west bank of the Jordan River. All the different kinds of violence are part of the *violence solution*.

The violence solution is very simple: "If something seems wrong, make it right by force." Strong emotions can lead to violence. Feelings of greed, anger, envy, hatred, or frustration are often handled with outbursts of violence. Fear can also cause violence. If someone is so afraid of being hurt or robbed or bothered, that person can think that using a handgun will solve the problem.

If you are hurt by your best friend, you may think that strong words or a punch in the mouth can solve the problem, too. There is a relationship between a military takeover in Poland, a street fight in the Bronx, and you throwing a plate of cold spaghetti at your little brother. All three of those actions are part of the violence solution.

The Peace Solution

Jesus knew what violence was all about. He saw violence in the streets of Israel. He saw bickering among His own Apostles. He saw how willing the leaders of the people were to use the violence solution—putting people to death by stoning in a public place and without a trial. Yet, Jesus said, "You have heard the commandment: 'An eye for an eye, a tooth for a tooth.' But what I say to you is: offer no resistance to injury. When a person strikes you on the right cheek, turn and offer the other cheek. If anyone wants to go to law over your shirt, hand over your coat as well. Should anyone press you into service for one mile, go for two miles.... Love your enemies, do good to those who hate you; bless those who curse you, and pray for those who maltreat you" *(Matthew 5:38–41; Luke 6:27–28).*

Jesus was not teaching His followers how to be weaklings. He was teaching those who believe in Him a new kind of strength—strength to stop the violence solution and use instead the *peace solution*. Throughout the history of the Church, the peace solution has been a very difficult lesson to learn.

Christians have been violent. They have fought wars and crusades. Protestants have fought Catholics. Catholics have fought Catholics. But there have always been followers of Jesus who have reminded everyone that the violence solution does not work.

On October 4, 1965—the feast day of Saint Francis who is the saint of peace—Pope Paul VI traveled to the United Nations headquarters in New York. There, the frail man who had the very big job of leading the Catholic Church pleaded with leaders from all over the world. He said to them to stop using the violence solution. "No more war," said the pope. "War never again!" That message is just as true for you on the playground or in your living room as it is for the leaders of the world.

Peaceful Attitudes and Skills

To show the kind of love that Jesus taught, to stop the violence solution and use the peace solution, it helps to develop some peaceful attitudes and some peaceful skills. These attitudes and skills do not come overnight. But if you develop them, it will be easier for you to be kind and peaceful in your choices and actions.

First, here are three attitudes. Jesus taught them, but you can never repeat them too often.

1. *Blessed are the gentle.* Being violent is not strong or brave. It takes real courage and strength to be gentle with other people, no matter how easy it would seem to run them down or to hurt them.
2. *Blessed are the peacemakers.* To show kindness and love is to stop the violence solution. Everybody has the chance and the ability to find peaceful solutions when things go wrong.

3. *Blessed are those who hunger for what is right.* The followers of Jesus know that behind every act of violence is some other problem. The followers of Jesus, therefore, work to solve those problems. They know that it will be easier to stop the violence solution if the causes of violence are stopped, too.

Three simple skills can be developed to help you bring love and kindness to others—to use the peace solution:

1. *Communication.* Learn to recognize your own feelings and to express them to others. Learn that many violent actions might never have happened if the people involved had the ability to talk about what was going on inside.
2. *Compromise.* One of the best peacekeeping skills is learning that you cannot always have your own way. Most solutions to problems involve *giving* and giving in.
3. *Caring.* The more you are able to care about others, their needs, their feelings, and their hopes, the more likely you will be able to use the peace solution.

There are many other skills and attitudes you can learn which will help you act as a loving follower of Jesus. Every day, you have the chance to bring peace to others. If you are following Jesus and His message, you will remind people who look at you that "love is kind."

Questions

1. What is the violence solution?
2. What is the peace solution?
3. What are the attitudes and skills you can develop which will help you use the peace solution?
4. How do you react when you experience anger or another strong emotion? Describe your feelings and your reactions.

Activities

1. Collect two stories from the newspaper or television news which show the violence solution. In small groups, discuss how each situation could have turned out if someone had used the peace solution.
2. Read Romans 12:9–21. When you have finished, make a personal reminder based on what you read. The reminder should be a help to you when you get into situations that could be violent. Share what you have done with your family.

A Code of Peace

Bringing peace and kindness to others takes practice. Using what you have learned in this chapter, formulate your own code of conduct for using the peace solution in the way you act toward others.

First of all, review the skills and attitudes listed below. Then, change each one into a personal rule for yourself. Be as honest and as practical as you can be. When you have written your six rules, take two real or imaginary situations and describe how you would use your personal code to find a peace solution in each situation.

My Code of Peace, Love, and Kindness

1. Caring
2. Compromise
3. Communication
4. Gentleness
5. Peacemaking
6. Making things right

Review

Match the item in column B with the attitude or skill in column A which it best describes.

A	**B**
1. ___ Blessed are peacemakers.	a. "I want you to know that I am very angry."
2. ___ Caring	b. "I really want what is best for you."
3. ___ Communication	c. "Maybe we could take turns doing the chores."
4. ___ Blessed are the gentle.	d. "I really don't think fighting is going to solve anything between you two."
5. ___ Compromise	e. "I am not going to do anything to hurt you."

Projects

1. Make a litany-type prayer for peace. Have each person in the class write one short sentence about a situation in the world, the community, or the parish which needs the peace solution. Then, choose a response like "Lord, make us channels of Your peace," or "Lord, let us show Your kindness and Your love." Each student can read his or her sentence, and the whole class can pray the response together. If you wish, you can turn this peace litany into a prayer service by adding music and readings.

2. As an ongoing project, you can start a "Peace Watch" scrapbook or bulletin board. Divide the book or the display into two sections. On one section, put examples of the violence solution. On the other section, put examples of the peace solution. When the project is complete, share it with another class or with the whole parish.

3. As a family project, share what you have learned in this chapter with your family. Work together with your family to make a family code of peace.

Prayer

Rejoice in the Lord always! I say it again. Rejoice! Everyone should see how unselfish you are. The Lord is near. Dismiss all anxiety from your minds. Present your needs to God in every form of prayer and in petitions full of gratitude. Then God's own peace, which is beyond all understanding, will stand guard over your hearts and minds, in Christ Jesus.

(Philippians 4:4–7)

17

Love Is Not Selfish

In This Chapter

You will discover the importance of being unselfish when you love someone.

You will see that unselfish attitudes and skills can help you make right choices in your relationships with others.

You will experience ways of becoming more unselfish in your actions and relationships.

Have No Fear, Joseph

Joseph pushed the wood shavings around with his foot. He sat under the window of his tiny shop. He had promised Simeon the Farmer that he would have a new yoke made for the man's team of oxen, and today was the day he had promised it would be finished. "I really do love her," Joseph thought. "But this is not the way I had it planned. I thought we would get married, have a family, pray together, and celebrate the feasts. We would watch our children grow, and we would get old together. But what now?"

Joseph got up. He took a rasp in his hand and started to smooth out the curves of the yoke he had been making. Mary was going to have a baby. People were starting to talk behind her back. And then, there was the dream Joseph had last night. "Have no fear, Joseph," said a voice in the dream, "about taking Mary to be your wife. It is by the Holy Spirit that she is having the baby. She will have a son, and you will name Him Jesus because He will save the people."

Until he had that dream, Joseph thought he would just quietly stop the wedding. That way, nobody would think that Mary had broken any of the laws. But now, Joseph was confused all over again. He stopped scraping and walked over to the door of the shop. He lifted his dusty arm to his forehead to block out the afternoon sun. In the distance he saw Mary—beautiful Mary—walking to the well. "What am I doing?" Joseph said aloud. "I have been thinking about myself, my plans, my feelings, and my future. What about Mary? She must be frightened to death. She is the one who has to be confused. She is the one who is getting the curious stares."

Joseph threw down the rasp. He grabbed a cloth to wipe off his arms and face. "She is going to need

help," he thought. "She is going to need me. I am strong. I have a craft..."

With that, Joseph bolted out the shop door and across the square leaving a trail of afternoon dust. When he got to the well, he held Mary gently by the shoulders. He looked right into her eyes. "Mary," he said, "I don't understand what is happening. But whatever it is, I am sure of one thing. I love you. I will care for you. I will treat the child like my own. I trust that God will take care of the rest."

Before Mary could say anything in answer, Joseph swept up the water jar in his hands. Together Mary and Joseph walked back to Mary's house. Joseph knew of his love for Mary. What he did not know was that for the rest of human history, his little family would be called "holy."

Questions

1. Why was Joseph experiencing confusion?
2. What helped Joseph make his decision?
3. Have you ever forgotten about yourself because someone you care for needed you? How did you feel? What did you do?

Activities

1. In small groups, select one of the passages listed below. Read the passage and discuss what the passage teaches about relationships with other people. Then, make up a definition of *love* based on what you have read.
   a. Luke 5:17–20
   b. Luke 7:39–45
   c. John 2:1–10
   d. John 4:4–29
2. Select one article from a popular magazine or one program from television. Read or watch carefully what you have selected. When you have finished, write a definition of *love* based on what you have read or watched. If you wish, repeat this activity using a popular song.

How Does Love Feel?

 aydreams are wonderful things. In daydreams, dark jungles are explored, mountains climbed, and big games won with a single shot just as the clock runs out. The human imagination is a place where the impossible can happen—where the seeds of the future are planted. Your imagination is a gift from God in which you can look ahead, make plans, and explore possibilities.

On the other hand, the imagination can become a very selfish place. It can be the stage where you are always the star. It can be the stadium where you are always the hero. It can be the laboratory in which you make all the scientific breakthroughs. It can be the world in which you are always loved and cared for.

One question the imagination is always trying to answer for you is "How does love feel?" In looking for the answer to that question, you build dreams of romance, heroics, fancy cars, world travel, and feelings of pleasure. Sometimes, when you are trying to figure love out, your imagination can do you a disservice. Your imagination can keep the people in your daydreams faceless, unreal, far away.

As long as you are looking for the feelings of love with you in the center, you do not have the whole picture. Love is not found in the mirror. Combs, brushes, lotions, creams, clothes, and jewelry are not the tools of love. The answer to how does love feel is found hiding behind one beautiful and powerful word, *giving*.

Made for More

When Saint Joseph was growing up, he had the same dreams and plans every Jewish boy had. Mary shared the dreams and plans of every other Jewish girl. But God had something more in mind for these two young people. God's plans for Mary and Joseph did not take place by magic. The great miracle of the birth of Jesus started with two very human miracles. Mary gave herself to God. She said *yes* to His plans for her. Joseph gave himself to Mary and to Jesus. He said *yes* to God's plans for him. Those two gifts made it possible for Jesus to be born, to be cared for, to be made ready to spread His covenant of love.

God has plans for you, too. You are at an age when you start guessing and dreaming about the future. You experience a whole range of feelings about yourself and about others. You are curious about sex and sexual feelings. You wonder about your attractions to others. Sometimes, you may feel angry one minute and peaceful the next. Some days you are happy as a lark, and other days you feel like there is a cloud hanging over your head. With all these different feelings, it can be pretty difficult to focus on any kind of future at all.

Because of everything that is going on inside you now, you are ready to learn a very important lesson about love. The lesson you learn will have to grow and to deepen over the years. You will have many different experiences, many different relationships, and many different friends. But what you learn about love will help you make good choices in your relationships with others. The most important attitude toward love that any follower of Jesus can have is simply this: love is not selfish.

When it comes to relationships between boys and girls, this attitude can make the difference between real happiness and real misery. It seems like everybody puts a lot of importance on sex. Advertisers use it to sell jeans, cars, and even vegetables. Songs are written about it. Movies are made about it. People talk about sex all the time. It is almost as if sex is something outside a person—something that is meant for play or pleasure.

In the midst of all the talk and writing about sex, it is critical that a young Christian remember that love is not selfish. You cannot learn everything you need to know in your relationships with others in one religion class. But you can learn three simple skills, or steps, that can be your guides for growing in love: (1) know your feelings, (2) be informed, and (3) be full of care.

Know Your Feelings

The emotions and feelings you have as a human being are gifts from God. They are messages which help you recognize what is going on inside yourself. Feelings are neither good nor bad. Feelings just are. What you do with your feelings makes all the difference in the world. There is nothing wrong with getting angry when someone calls you a name. But if your anger has made you clench your fingers into a fist, take a roundhouse swing, and bloody that person's nose, you have chosen to do something destructive with your anger. There is nothing particularly right about feeling sad when a friend's grandmother dies. But if that feeling leads you to spend time with your friend and offer your support, you have done something constructive with your sadness.

The difference between animals and humans when it comes to sexual feelings is very important. Sexual feeling in animals has one purpose—to produce offspring. In humans, sexual feelings help people learn how to form lasting bonds with others. Sexual feelings help people learn more about the kind of giving and sacrifice that is a part of really loving someone. So, a very important skill that you can develop is the habit of recognizing and dealing with your feelings.

Be Informed

To keep your love from being selfish, you need to know what relationships with others are all about. You need to have good, accurate, and honest information about your body and the bodies of others. You need to know, too, what rules your Church has about relationships with others. If you were going to sail across the Atlantic Ocean by yourself, you would want to know everything you could about the ship in which you would travel. You would study the currents, the weather, and the wind. You would learn all the possible safety and survival techniques, too. You would want to be sure of how to respond if something went wrong.

You are going on a much more serious journey—the journey of loving others. It is very important that you know about yourself, about the problems you might encounter, and about what to do if somehow you go wrong. It is critical that you get this information from people you can trust—people who share your attitude that love is not selfish. Parents, teachers, pastors, and counselors are all willing to give you the kind of information you need for your journey. And remember the sacrament of Reconciliation, too. That is a special help for you to seek forgiveness when something has gone wrong and to seek advice to keep things going right.

Be Full of Care

Once, when some of the enemies of Jesus wanted to trap Him, they brought to Him a woman who had been caught committing *adultery*. There was an ancient law which said that anyone caught committing that sin should be stoned to death in a public place. The enemies of Jesus wanted to see if He would break that ancient law.

The poor woman was terrified. She was crying for shame and fear. At first, Jesus did not look at her. He simply said, "Let the one among you who has not sinned, throw the first stone." Then, Jesus waited. While He waited, he doodled in the sand with His finger. One by one, the people who had brought the woman dropped their stones and went away.

Jesus looked at the woman who was still quivering in terror. He took her by the hand and helped her to her feet. "Where did they all go?" Jesus asked her. "Has no one condemned you?"

Adultery An act of unfaithfulness on the part of a husband or wife. Adultery is a very serious sin against the Law of God and the laws of the Church.

"No one, sir," the woman answered, holding back a sob.

"I do not condemn you either," Jesus said to the woman. "You may go. But from now on, avoid this sin."

Jesus was being careful—*full of care*. He did not look down on what the woman had done. He did not think that it was a good and nasty bit of gossip. He did not tell her how dangerous it was to be involved in sinful relationships. He simply cared.

As you grow in the attitude that love is not selfish, remember that followers of Jesus do not use people. Instead, they care for people. They remember the words of Jesus. They remember the example of Joseph and Mary and other believers. Before you make any decisions or choices in your relationships with others, ask yourself this question: "If people see what I am about to do or hear what I am about to say, will they get the message that love is not selfish?"

Questions

1. What is the most basic attitude Christians have in their relationships with others?
2. What are three skills that help a person make loving choices in his or her relationships with others? Give one example of each skill.
3. What is one of your dreams for the future? How can the three skills mentioned in this chapter help you make that dream a reality?

Activities

1. One way to be uncaring about people is to give them labels which put people down. Sometimes, these labels are called stereotypes. List three labels that boys sometimes give girls. Then, list three labels that girls sometimes give boys. Share your lists with the class. Make a master list and select the top five labels for each. Then, discuss how labels can mean that people do not know their feelings, are not informed, or are not full of care.

2. Make a personal reminder in the form of a bookmark or wall sign which will make you more aware of the fact that God has plans for you. Choose thoughts from this chapter to help you make the reminder. Share it with your family. Display it somewhere you will see it often.

Growing in Unselfishness

When you were very young, you were the center of your universe. That is as it should be because you were getting used to being alive and being a person. But now, you are growing up. You are not the center of the universe anymore. You are learning new ways of being yourself and still reaching out to other people. For you to remain as selfish as you were when you were very young can be as embarrassing as being a grown-up who still sleeps with a teddy bear or still uses a Donald Duck toothbrush.

Use the three skills for choosing you learned in this chapter to help you grow in unselfishness. Pick three people in your life. These people do not have to be people with whom you have a girl-boy friendship. They can be parents, brothers, sisters, friends—anybody at all. Then, following the chart below as a guide, ask three questions of yourself: (1) What are my real feelings about this person? (2) What information do I need? and (3) How can I be more caring toward this person? Keep your answers private. When you have finished, write one resolution you can make which will help you be more unselfish. Share your resolution with the class.

Person	Feelings	Information	Caring
1.			
2.			
3.			

My caring resolution is

Review

Circle the T if the statement is true. Circle the F if the statement is false.

1. Daydreams are a waste of time.   T   F

2. It is wrong to be curious or to wonder how it feels to be in love.   T   F

3. It is important to remember that relationships between boys and girls are always selfish.   T   F

4. Jesus gave examples of what it means to be careful in relationships.   T   F

5. In trying to follow Christian love, too much honest and accurate information is dangerous.   T   F

Projects

1. As a class, rate the top-ten songs on how well they show that love is not selfish. Using the entertainment section of your newspaper or of some popular magazine, write the title of each of the top-ten hits on the board. Someone who knows the lyrics can give the class a summary. Then, the class can vote a "love is not selfish" rating of from one to ten (ten being best) for each song. Share your rating with other classes.

2. Read Matthew 2:18–24 and Luke 1:26–55. In small groups, plan ways in which the class can celebrate the unselfish love of Joseph and Mary—art, prayer, music, song, or the like. Bring the matter before the whole class and then put together a special celebration.

Prayer

Father and Creator of all things, who gave us an example of love and work in Saint Joseph, grant that through his help and prayers, we may follow the plans You have for us and receive the rewards You promised.

(Prayer for the Feast of Saint Joseph)

18

Love Is Honest

In This Chapter

You will discover that honesty is an important part of the love commandment of Jesus.

You will learn what it means to be an honest and just person.

You will experience ways in which you can become more honest and just.

An Honest Answer

How good are you at giving an honest answer? Most people try to be honest. But being honest is not always as simple as it sounds. Carefully read the five situations listed below. On a separate sheet of paper, write three answers to each of the situations. Briefly describe what will happen if the person does or says what you suggest. Put a star in front of the answer you think is the most honest. Discuss each situation in class. Share your personal answers and try to select what the class considers the most honest answer for each situation.

1. Carol forgot to study for her math test. She is very frightened that she will fail. From where she is sitting, she can see both Rodrigo's and Connie's work. Rodrigo is a much better student than Connie. What should Carol do?

2. Philip makes ten dollars a week passing out handbills in his neighborhood. One week, Philip forgot to pass them out. He is very embarrassed about forgetting. On Friday, his manager gives Philip the ten dollars. What should Philip do?

3. Grant went to the supermarket for his father. While shopping, he slipped a candy bar into his pocket. By the time he reached the check stand, he was having second thoughts, but anything he did now would look pretty silly. What should Grant do?
4. Sarah invited Mindy to a party. Mindy really does not want to go. But she does not want to hurt Sarah's feelings either. What should Mindy say?
5. Charlene knows that the new regulations for using the school gym have been posted on the main bulletin board. Charlene wants to practice her jump shot during free period. She is afraid that might not be allowed anymore. What should Charlene do?

Questions

1. Which of the situations was the hardest for you to answer? Which was the easiest? Why?
2. How difficult was it for the class to decide on the most honest answer? Why do you think some arguments developed?
3. How important is honesty to you?

Activities

1. In small groups, make up one situation like the ones presented here. Then, act out the situation for the rest of the class. The class can then work out an honest answer for each situation.
2. Search through newspapers and magazines and television news for an example of honesty and of dishonesty in (a) business, (b) politics, (c) family, or (d) sports. Report on what you have discovered.

Being Whole

It may seem quite strange at first to talk about honesty as a way of loving other people. Yet, without honesty, it is impossible to tell if your love for others is real and sincere.

When the Israelites were wandering in the desert, honesty was a matter of survival. If someone were to steal someone else's camel or tent or water, the other person could die in the severe climate. In addition, lying, stealing, cheating, or desiring what belonged to someone else could have caused great mistrust, hatred, and fear among God's People as they fought the terrible desert sands. So, the punishment for dishonesty was swift and very harsh. For stealing, a person could lose his or her hand. For lying, a person could be sent away from camp—a punishment that often meant death.

When God gave Moses the commandments on Mount Sinai, three of those commandments had to do with honesty: "You shall not steal. You shall not bear false witness. You shall not covet your neighbor's goods." Now, honesty meant more than survival. Honesty was part of the Israelites' identity as God's People.

When Jesus was teaching about the Father's love, He often taught about honesty, truth, and the trust that honesty brings.

> "If you can trust a person in little things, you can also trust that person in greater; while anyone unjust in a slight matter is also unjust in greater. If you cannot be trusted with elusive wealth, who will trust you with lasting? And if you have not been trustworthy with someone else's money, who will give you what is to be your own?"
>
> *(Luke 16:10–12)*

Jesus told His followers to say yes when they mean yes and no when they mean no (see Matthew 5:37). And at the Last Supper, when Jesus was giving His disciples a final instruction in the new commandment of love, He prayed to the Father:

"For these I pray—
consecrate them by means of truth—
Your word is truth.
As You have sent Me into the world,
so I have sent them into the world;
I consecrate Myself for their sakes now,
that they may be consecrated in truth."

(John 17:17–19)

Consecrate   To make holy. When the priest consecrates the bread and wine at Mass, they become the Body and Blood of Christ.

In the new covenant, honesty is a sign that the followers of Jesus are hearers and doers of God's own truth. And so, honesty is both an attitude and a skill. It is an attitude because it colors the way people look at things—open, aware, and unafraid of the truth. It is a skill because it is a habitual way of acting—direct, straightforward, and unafraid of saying and doing what is right.

Honesty in Attitude

In the Christian heart, the truth is a friend and an ally. "I want the truth" is a sentence that is often said but not always meant. When the sick person looks at the doctor and asks for the truth, he or she may face some very frightening news. When the young ballet student asks for the truth about his or her talent, the teacher might say that there is not enough talent there at all.

But hardest of all is for you to look in the mirror and say, "I want the truth." A person who is honest in attitude does not lie to him or herself. When you are honest in attitude, you want to know yourself and what you are all about. You do not want to kid yourself into thinking that you are more or less than you really are. Jesus knew that His first followers were very unsure of themselves. They were being hassled by their friends and neighbors. They were being kidded and teased. So, Jesus said to them, "If you live according to My teaching, you are truly My disciples; then you will know the truth, and the truth will set you free" *(John 8:31–32)*.

When the sick person knows the truth about his or her disease, the process of healing can begin. When the student of ballet knows the truth about talent, he or she can freely plan the future. When you look in the mirror and are honest with yourself, you are free to be honest, kind, unselfish, and patient with others.

The Skill of Honesty

If you have ever met someone who always lies, you understand just how hard it is to take the person seriously. These liars create a whole fantasy world in which to live. What they have is always the best. They always meet famous people. They never do anything wrong. They always have an excuse. They often put other people down. They live in a liar's prison. With every lie, they add another brick to the jail. With every dishonest action, they put another bar in the window. Every time they cheat or steal, they make themselves more comfortable in their cells.

Learning the skills of honesty is a way to avoid liar's prison. Even if you have not learned these skills yet, there is always hope because with God's help, with the help of the sacraments, and the support of others, there is always a parole available for people who are seeking the truth.

Listed below are four things to remember as you develop the skill of honesty. The first two have to do with the way you speak, and the second two have to do with the way you act.

1. *Say what you mean.* Develop the habit of saying clearly and openly what you mean to say. Try very hard not to hide behind words. One way to help yourself say what you mean is to think carefully

before you speak. Ask yourself the meaning of the words you are about to use and the effect your words will have on others. While someone's clumsiness may be a fact, it would not be honest to use that clumsiness as a weapon by saying, "Boy, you are the clumsiest person I have ever met." Such a sentence can only hurt.

2. *Mean what you say.* It is very easy to become a chameleon. The chameleon is an animal that changes color to blend in with any surroundings. A human chameleon says what he or she thinks will please people right now. With good people, they speak nicely. With boasters, they boast. With liars, they lie. Jesus was pretty hard on human chameleons. He called them hypocrites, people who say one thing but do another.

3. *Act with respect for people's property.* The honest person has as much care for the property of others as for his or her own property. What a person has is a little part of what they are. If you take or break a person's property, the message you give is one of disrespect for that person.

4. *Act with respect for people's rights.* Everybody has rights. Everybody has the right to life, to a good reputation, to be happy, and to be themselves. Honest people are very aware of the rights of others. And in their actions, honest people are very careful not to harm or take those rights away.

A Minister of Honesty

"Nuns should not be jailers!" said the young sister as she stood before the *chancellor's* desk. Her face was calm, but the priest had no doubt that this sister meant business.

"The Convent of the Refuge is a disgrace, Father," the sister continued. "It should be called the women's prison of Angers. The young women are locked up. There is no help for them. We give them bibles, beds, and meals, and expect to make a difference. But unless we are honest and open with them, we will make no change."

Chancellor A peson who assists the bishop in the running of a diocese. The chancellor helps carry on the business side of caring for the Catholics in a specific area.

"Now, Sister," said the priest, "be reasonable. These girls are criminals. They have robbed, lied, cheated, stolen, and committed every manner of crime. The only reason these runaways are at the Refuge and not in jail is because they are too young. Now, go back and tell your sisters that I am aware of their good work . . ."

"No!" said Sister Mary Euphrasia Pelletier. "It is God's will that we treat these girls with kindness. He would have it no other way. They need help. They need loving and caring people who will be honest and open with them. Then, when the day comes for a girl to leave the Refuge, she will feel like a person. She will feel loved. She will see the value of living inside the law."

When Mary Euphrasia was only twenty-nine years old, she was made the sister superior of the Refuge in Angers. Refuges had been established throughout France two centuries earlier. But by 1826, they had become little more than prisons. What Sister Mary Euphrasia began in the chancellor's office in Angers became a whole religious movement—the Sisters of the Good Shepherd.

By the time Sister Mary Euphrasia died, there were over 2,700 Good Shepherd sisters working to help and to rehabilitate young women all over the world. Today, Saint Mary Euphrasia watches over the work her sisters are doing in almost every nation in the world. The Good Shepherd sisters work to help young women discover the truth because the truth will set them free.

Questions

1. How did honesty grow from a matter of survival to a sign of love? Describe the process briefly.
2. How is honesty both a skill and an attitude?
3. What does it mean that "the truth will set you free"?
4. What are the steps in developing the skill of honesty?

Activities

1. In small groups, read and discuss the message Jesus had for people who were human chameleons—hypocrites. You will find the story in Matthew 23:1–29. Discuss why Jesus was so hard on hypocrites.

2. Make a list of motives. Divide a sheet of paper into two columns. In one column, write three reasons for telling the truth. In the other column, write three reasons people give for lying. Share your individual lists with the class. Try to select the top five motives in each category. Share what the class has done with your family.

Practicing Honest Love

Nobody can learn to be honest for you. Honesty is something that you have to learn and to develop on your own. But in the Christian community, it is important for the followers of Jesus to support one another in their efforts to show that love is honest. To help that process along, use the two charts given below as guides. The first should be private. The second should be a group activity.

1. *How honest are you?* Think quietly about each attitude and skill before you answer.

Attitudes and Skills	How Honest Am I?
1. I want to know the truth.	
2. Say what you mean.	
3. Mean what you say.	
4. Respect others' things.	
5. Respect others' rights.	

2. *Group support.* Now, for each attitude and skill, describe a real or imaginary situation in which that kind of honesty is needed. Then, briefly describe how you could help and support one another in honesty if that situation occurs.

Attitude and Skills	Situation	Group Support
1. I want to know the truth.		
2. Say what you mean.		
3. Mean what you say.		
4. Respect others' things.		
5. Respect others' rights.		

Review

Fill in the missing words.

1. For the Israelites, honesty was a matter of ___ .

2. Jesus asked the Father to ___ His followers in truth.

3. "The truth will set you ___ ."

4. Honesty is both an ___ and a ___ .

5. Jesus called people ___ who did not mean what they said.

Projects

1. Make a class code of honesty. Work first in small groups. Form five statements that you feel would be good rules to help the class show that love is honest. Be sure there is agreement in the group. When everyone has finished making their statements, share them with the whole class. Vote for the ten best statements.

2. Make an honesty survey. Each student can ask two people outside the class what they mean by honesty. Report on the findings.

3. Share what you have learned about honest love with your family. If possible, do the group-support exercise with your family. You may want to make a family code of honesty, too.

Prayer

O God, dear Lord, teach us the speech
with which to ask Your blessings.
This day, this night, in dark and light,
we thank You for all Your gifts.

Dear God, may we do no bad deed
and to Your teachings always be true.
May we forever breathe the breath of Your love
and every moment be aware of Your presence above.

(Pakistani children's prayer)

Reviewing Part Three

Summary

In this Part, you have learned several truths about your Catholic Faith.

1. Catholic Christians take responsibility for their moral actions and choices. They build their houses on rock.
2. Original sin and personal sin are real, and it is at times a real struggle to do what is right. It is helpful to develop virtues—good habits of acting.
3. Christian love is patient. It does not just look for the easy solutions to problems. It looks for the right solutions to problems.
4. Kindness and peacefulness are signs of the new covenant of love. For the Christian, violence is not a ready answer for difficulties. Kindness is the Christian answer.
5. In relationships with others, Catholic Christians want to develop attitudes of unselfishness.
6. Honesty is a sign of sincere and open love for others. Followers of Jesus seek the truth because the truth will set them free.

Questions

1. What does it mean to build your house on rock?
2. What is your conscience?
3. Why do people make excuses for making wrong choices? What is behind those excuses?

4. What are the four qualities of patient love?
5. In your own words, what is the lesson of the parable of the fig tree?
6. What are the three attitudes and the three skills you can develop to help you use the peace solution?
7. What is the most basic attitude Christians should have in their relationships with others?
8. What are three skills that help a person make loving choices in his or her relationships with others?
9. How is honesty both a skill and an attitude?
10. What are the steps in developing the virtue of honesty?

True or False

Circle the T if the statement is true. Circle the F if the statement is false.

1. Mastering Christian skills is a way to build your house on rock.	T	F
2. You have a responsibility for making sure that your conscience is in good working order.	T	F
3. For a good person, there is never any struggle in living up to the Gospel.	T	F
4. It is important to have a personal plan of action for putting Jesus' love commandment into your life.	T	F
5. The use of alcohol or drugs is never a way of escaping responsibility.	T	F
6. Patience is one of the major excuses for not loving others.	T	F
7. Gentleness is a kind of strength.	T	F

8. It is important to be informed about human
   relationships.   T   F
9. Knowing your feelings is a good way to become more
   selfish.   T   F
10. A truly honest person is not afraid of the truth. T   F

Matching

Match the item in column B which best identifies each
person in column A.

A

1. ____ Saint Monica
2. ____ Saint Ignatius
3. ____ Matt Talbot
4. ____ Sister Maura Clarke
5. ____ Saint Joseph
6. ____ Saint Mary Euphrasia

B

a. A person who put his own plans
   aside for the one he loved
b. A person who helped show that
   love is honest
c. A soldier who learned Christian
   responsibility
d. A person who prayed that her
   son would build on rock
e. A person who turned from
   alcohol to a life which showed
   that love is patient
f. A person whose kindness was
   rewarded with the violence
   solution

Vocabulary

Use the following terms in a sentence.

ethics	addiction
attitude	virtue
original sin	skill
vice	gentleness

Celebration

Plan a special prayer service or a class Mass to celebrate what you have learned about the signs of the covenant. Use prayers, readings, and ideas from this Part of the book. Set aside a special time for the Mass or service. Remember, your celebration should show the importance of building on rock, the struggle to be responsible, and the fact that love is patient, kind, unselfish, and honest. Pages 284–285 of your Handbook will help you with your plans. Be sure to include music and actions.

I received from the Lord what I handed on to you, namely, that the Lord Jesus on the night in which He was betrayed took bread, and after He had given thanks, broke it and said, "This is My Body, which is for you. Do this in remembrance of Me."

(1 Corinthians 11:23–24)

PART FOUR

A Family of Believers

19

Together in Christ Jesus

In This Chapter

You will discover that the followers of Jesus form one living Body.

You will recall how this Body is nourished and strengthened by the Eucharist.

You will learn ways you can participate in the Eucharist.

The Old Tree

hen the administrator of the hospital asked Orville Alexander if he wanted something special for his one hundredth birthday, she was not prepared for the answer she got. "I want to visit my tree!" Orville said.

Four days later, the car pulled up to the old Victorian house. This was the house where Orville was born. The first floor had been divided into a barbershop and a florist. The second floor held the law offices of Michaels, Gould, and Davis. But Orville was not interested in the house.

Before the driver could turn off the engine, Orville opened the car door, grabbed his cane, and headed for the tree. The backyard had become a pool of asphalt. But in the center of the pool stood a huge sprawling oak like a defiant island.

The tree had been planted the day Orville was born. Hiram Alexander, Orville's father, was so excited when his first boy was born that he planted a tree to mark the day. The tree had witnessed Orville's life. The old man walked right up to the old oak with the firm familiarity a person might show greeting an old friend on the street.

Orville touched the tree. He could almost feel the sap running up the giant trunk and into the limbs, branches, and leaves. With the sap ran the memories. The straight young tree saw Orville playing tag in the yard. The early shade covered the young man as he read stories of daring and adventure on a summer afternoon.

Five feet from the ground were the faded initials Orville had carved as a message of love for Martha. And under the sturdy tree, Martha and Orville had celebrated their wedding. To the tree Orville came shedding tears at the death of Hiram. Ten years later, Orville came to cry again for the death of his mother.

The tree was a survivor and so was Orville. Orville saw the tree's scar from the fire of 1937. His family had almost lost the house and the tree. He reached up and touched a blackened stump of a limb where lightning had struck in 1925. Orville smiled at his tree.

The tree loved to celebrate births. Each of Orville's five children had played by the tree. Each of them had celebrated birthdays, holidays, graduations, and marriages in the presence of the tree. As Orville's eyes scanned the tree, he saw again the rope for the swing, the Japanese lanterns hung from the boughs, the crepe paper dangling from the twigs, and the children climbing through the dome of leaves.

Orville smiled. Everything had changed. The neighborhood was different. The city had gobbled it up and hidden it in piles of concrete and steel. The world was different—faster and somewhat harder to handle. The family had scattered. Children had moved away. Grandchildren had become hard to remember. Great-grandchildren hardly knew that Orville existed. But the tree remembered.

Orville turned slowly. He gave the old tree a final pat. Then, he walked to the car, without looking back. "I am happy," Orville said to no one in particular, "because the tree remembers."

Questions

1. Why was the old tree so important to Orville Alexander?
2. Why did Orville want to visit the tree?
3. What are some traditions or customs you or your family have which help you remember who you are?

Activities

1. In small groups, select one of the passages listed below. Read the passage in the group and discuss how the passage tells you who you are.
   a. Matthew 13:31–33—two parables
   b. Matthew 19:19–20—powerful prayer
   c. Luke 12:33–36—the story of the lamp
2. Ask your grandparents, parents, or other older adults to tell you one of their happiest childhood memories. Record the memory in story form and share it with the class. Discuss what you have shared.

The Body of Christ

On a hill outside Jerusalem, the Father planted a tree. Hanging from the tree of the cross, Jesus was giving up His life. But death would not be the end of Jesus. Jesus was going to rise again. From the tree the Father planted, many, many branches were going to reach out.

After Pentecost, the tree began to grow. The fresh new branches spread with the teaching and sharing of the Apostles to the towns and villages around Jerusalem. Wherever the Apostles went, people believed in Jesus, accepted baptism, and gathered around the table to celebrate the Lord's Supper.

The branches reached out. One branch settled in Antioch, Syria. Here the followers of Jesus were first called Christians. In Antioch, the community shared everything they owned. They studied and prayed. They, too, were held together by celebrating the Eucharist. The Christians of Antioch appointed men and women to care for the sick, to teach, to carry food to the poor, to lead, and to administer the material possessions of the believers.

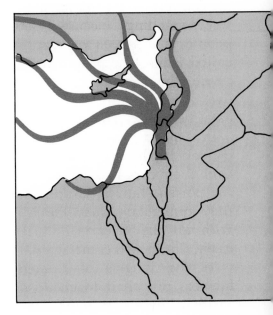

A branch settled in Alexandria, in Egypt. Here the Apostles and bishops used the customs and learning of this North African center to help the people understand the teachings of Jesus. Again the believers were baptized. Again they tried to love one another and came together to celebrate Mass.

The tree the Father had planted was growing larger and larger. It spread to Corinth, to Athens, to Milan, to Rome. The Holy Spirit was working in the Apostles, the deacons, the bishops, and the priests. Every believing person was like a fresh leaf on God's tree.

Saint Paul explained it to the people of Corinth in a very simple way:

"The body is one and has many members, but all the members, many though they are, are one body; and so it is with Christ. It was in one Spirit that all of us, whether Jew or Greek, slave or free, were baptized in one Body. All of us have been given to drink of the one Spirit."

(1 Corinthians 12:12–14)

The Tree Survives

The tree which the Father planted—the Body of Christ — is still alive. But the tree has scars. From the earliest days, people were not faithful. There have been *schisms* and separations. There have been wars within the Body. People have disagreed about how Christianity is to be lived. But in every age, people have gathered again to remember the center of the Body—the trunk of the tree—Jesus Christ.

In Russia, a bearded priest stands before a cloth-draped table. He is surrounded by the smoke of sweet-smelling incense. Between him and the people is a screen of beautifully painted pictures called icons. The people are singing, "The mercy of peace, the sacrifice of praise..." The priest bends over a plate of bread and a cup of wine. "Take and eat," he sings. "This is My Body."

In Poland, workers leave their homes at four o'clock in the morning. They tug their collars up over their ears to keep out the cold. They pack into the parish church. As they gather around the altar, they remember what life is all about. They sing with all their hearts, "Christ has died, Christ is risen, Christ will come again."

In the jungles of Guatemala, simple banana farmers pile their machetes outside the tiny room. Inside, they sit on mats and listen to the story of Jesus. Then, with the sounds of revolution ringing in the mountains nearby, the Guatemalans join hands and pray, "Lord Jesus Christ, You said to Your Apostles: I leave you peace, My peace I give to you. Look not on our sins, but on the faith of Your Church, and grant us the peace and unity of Your kingdom where You live forever and ever."

In a classroom in Philadelphia, six junior-high-school students are staying after school to help plan

Schism A separation or a division in the Church. A schism is caused when groups in the Church have a serious disagreement and cannot settle it. There is a schism between the Orthodox and Catholic Christians.

a class Eucharist. One of them pages through the book of readings. Another is writing a litany prayer. A third is choosing music that the whole class can sing. At eight o'clock tomorrow, the whole class will gather around the altar in the parish church and say, "Give us this day our daily bread and forgive us our trespasses as we forgive those who trespass against us."

Every time you celebrate the Eucharist, you are gathering in the shade of the tree the Father planted. You are remembering the teachings of Jesus. You are getting together with other members of the Body to keep the tree alive—to make sure that you are being faithful.

Just as the sharing and remembering and celebrating you do at home help to strengthen your family tree, the sharing you do at Mass strengthens your membership in the Body of Christ. At Mass, you are important. You are a part of the living Church. Even though you may sometimes feel a million miles away or bored or tired or sad, you are with other members of the Body.

As you pray the prayers, listen to the readings, sing the songs, and share in Communion, you are part of everything that has gone before. You are remembering the day the tree was planted on Calvary. You are a part of what happened at Antioch, Alexandria, Rome, and Corinth. You are part of what is happening in Russia, Poland, Guatemala, and Philadelphia. You are showing your pride and happiness to be one with others in Christ Jesus.

Questions

1. What were some of the activities the early Christians shared?
2. How did Saint Paul explain the Church to the people of Corinth?
3. What is one way that the tree has survived throughout the centuries?
4. What does the Eucharist mean to you?

Activities

1. Make a drawing of a tree. On the drawing, put symbols of how you are a member of the Body of Christ. Share your drawing with the class. Explain your symbols. Share the drawing with your family, too.
2. Select one of the passages from Saint Paul listed below. Read the passage. Then, write one sentence showing what the passage tells about being a member of the Body of Christ. Discuss what you have written.
   a. Romans 12:9—20
   b. Ephesians 5:8—14
   c. Colossians 3:12—17

A Eucharistic Community

Together with other members of the Body of Christ, you celebrate belonging every time you come together for the Eucharist. You are fed by the Eucharist in many different ways. Listed below are several important parts of the Mass. Using the chart as a guide, carefully review each part of the Mass that is listed. Then, for each part, describe how it reminds you of your membership in the Body of Christ. Describe what the part means to you. Finally, describe how you can help one another be more aware of your membership in the Eucharistic community. Discuss the results in class.

Part of Mass	Membership	Meaning	Greater Awareness
1. Entrance			
2. Gospel reading			
3. Profession of Faith			
4. Giving gifts			
5. Sign of peace			
6. Communion			

Review

Read each of the statements below. Then, rate each from 1 to 6. The number *1* means "I totally agree," and the number *6* means "I totally disagree." The other numbers show shades in between.

1. I am aware that I am a member of the Body of Christ.

   1   2   3   4   5   6

2. Every member of the Body of Christ is important.

    1   2   3   4   5   6

3. Jesus Christ is alive and present in the Church today.

    1   2   3   4   5   6

4. Preparing for and participating at Mass shows how much I appreciate my membership in the Body of Christ.

    1   2   3   4   5   6

5. There are ways we can help one another get more out of the Eucharistic Celebration.

    1   2   3   4   5   6

Projects

1. Keep an "awareness log." For one day, keep track of how many times you are aware that you are a member of the Body of Christ. What reminded you? Divide the reminders into the following categories: *(a)* people, *(b)* things, *(c)* events, and *(d)* yourself. Discuss what you have discovered by keeping the log.

2. Read the description Jesus gave of the vine and the branches (John 15:1–8). Then, make a poster, a banner, or a bulletin-board display showing how your parish is a branch of the vine. Share what you have done with the whole parish.

Prayer

Father, we celebrate the memory of Your Son.
We, Your people and Your ministers,
recall His passion,
His resurrection from the dead,
and His ascension into glory;
and from the many gifts You have given us
we offer to You, God of glory and majesty,
this holy and perfect sacrifice;
the bread of life and the cup of eternal salvation.

(Eucharistic Prayer I)

20

Born of Water and Spirit

In This Chapter

You will review how Baptism, Confirmation, and Eucharist are sacraments of belonging to the Body of Christ.

You will discover how to be more aware of your membership.

You will see how you practice membership by the way you act.

A Meeting with Jesus

icodemus carefully closed the gate to his garden. He made sure that it made no noise because he wanted to avoid disturbing the household. Then, Nicodemus adjusted his clothes over his face so that no one would recognize him. He walked quickly down the street of the basket weavers and ducked through the alley of the camel drivers. Soon, he was at the olive orchard at the edge of town. The bright moonlight and the gentle breeze sent a splatter of shadows through the orchard.

If the other members of the *Sanhedrin* knew where Nicodemus was going, they would be very angry with him. But Nicodemus really wanted to believe—he really wanted to know the truth. Nicodemus took a deep breath. Jesus was sitting on the stone bench by the well. He was waiting just as He said He would be. Nicodemus sat down next to Jesus.

"Rabbi," Nicodemus said, "we know you are a teacher come from God, for no one can perform signs and wonders such as You perform unless God is there . . ."

Jesus looked at Nicodemus and said, "No one can see the reign of God unless he or she is born from above."

Nicodemus was puzzled. "How can people be born again once they are old?" questioned Nicodemus. "Can they return to their mothers' wombs and be born over again?"

Jesus replied, "No one can enter God's kingdom without being born of water and the Spirit."

"How can this happen?" asked Nicodemus.

Jesus answered, "You hold the office of teacher of Israel and still you do not understand these matters? God so loved the world that He gave His only Son, that whoever believes in Him may not die but

Sanhedrin A Jewish court at the time of Jesus. The Sanhedrin answered questions about Jewish law.

may have eternal life. Those who practice evil hate the light and do not come near it for fear their deeds will be exposed. But those who act in truth come into the light, to make clear that their deeds are done in God."

Nicodemus never forgot that meeting with Jesus. He remembered it on that awful Friday when he came out into the light to provide the body of Jesus with a tomb. He remembered it, too, when he was born again of water and the Spirit—when he became a member of the Body of Christ.

Questions

1. Why was Nicodemus afraid to meet Jesus in public?
2. What was the meaning of the message Jesus gave Nicodemus?
3. When were you born of water and the Spirit? What does that mean for you?

Activities

1. Read the whole story of the meeting between Jesus and Nicodemus (John 3:1–21). In your own words, describe what Nicodemus might have been thinking when he heard the words of Jesus?

2. In small groups, make a list of all the parts you remember of a baptism ceremony. After you have listed three or four parts of the ceremony, discuss what each means to you and the group.

Christian Initiation

Every eye in the stadium was on the judges. All of Montreal and all of the world was dazzled by the performance of the young gymnast. There was a hush as the scorecards went up. "Ten, ten, ten, ten, ten!" For the first time in modern Olympic history, a gymnast had gotten a perfect score. The gold medal and the hearts of the world went to Nadia Comaneci.

Nadia was born on November 12, 1961, in Onesti, Romania. Her father was a mechanic. Her mother worked in an office. When she was just six years old, Nadia wanted to become a gymnast. So, she entered a program of training.

Nadia worked to learn the basics. She practiced her skills every day. Because she wanted to be the best, she never gave up. She had to make many sacrifices to work so hard, but Nadia knew how much she had to learn and how much she had to practice. In two years, she was chosen to be on the Junior National Team. After four more years, Nadia was chosen to be a member of the Romanian Olympic Team. In the summer Olympic Games of 1976, Nadia Comaneci won two gold medals, one silver medal, and the title of Women's World Champion.

The day after she returned to Romania from Canada, Nadia was seen walking to the gym to practice. She knew that even though she had been chosen and had won, she needed to work out every single day.

Christian Training

The *Rite of Christian Initiation of Adults* shows that becoming a member of the Body of Christ is a process. Everyone who joins the Church goes through a series of steps very similar to the ones Nadia took in becoming an Olympic gymnast. Part of taking these steps is the celebration of three

Rite of Christian Initiation of Adults The process by which a person joins the Catholic Church. This particular process is for people who are old enough to make up their own minds. Infants who are baptized go through a slightly different process.

sacraments—Baptism, Confirmation, and First Eucharist. The chart below shows the steps that Nadia took. Then, it shows the steps in the process of Christian initiation for adults. Finally, it shows the meaning of each step for the followers of Jesus.

Nadia's Steps	Christian Initiation	Meaning
1. She signed up for gymnastics.	The precatechumenate	A time of beginning and of questioning. (The word *catechumenate* means "instruction.")
2. She learned and practiced the basics.	The catechumenate	A period for learning the basics of the Christian faith. A time to start thinking and acting like a Christian.
3. She was chosen for the team, and she wins the Olympics.	The *election:* the new Christian receives the sacraments of Baptism, Confirmation, and First Eucharist.	A time for being proud and happy to belong to the Body of Christ and to become a full member.
4. She went back to the gym to practice some more.	*Mystagogia:* after-Baptism instructions	A time for the new member to make sure that he or she really can think and act like a member of the Body.

Your Steps

Most likely, you were baptized when you were a baby. You began your training with the sacrament of Baptism. But you still went through a series of steps. You gradually learned about the basics of your faith. You learned from your family. You learned by going to church. You learned by asking questions. When you were old enough, you began special classes in your faith. Every year, you learned a little more about what it means to be a member of the Body of Christ.

When you were old enough and when you could recognize that the bread and wine becomes Jesus, you were allowed to make your First Communion and your first confession, too. You learned more and

Election The step in Christian initiation when the new member is chosen to receive the sacraments of Baptism, Confirmation, and First Eucharist.

Mystagogia A time of special celebration and instruction for a newly baptized Catholic. The word *mystagogia* means "sharing the mysteries."

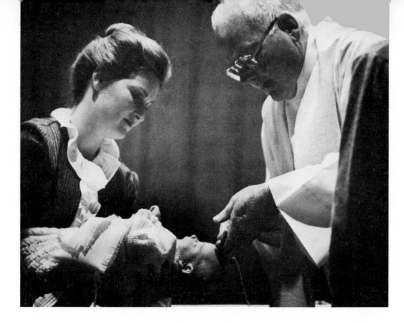

more about how members of the Body of Christ believe and act.

In the sacrament of Confirmation, you receive the Gift of the Holy Spirit in a special way, and you become a full and complete member of the team. But even after you are chosen to be confirmed, you still have learning and growing to do so that you do not forget the basics of being a Christian. You are reminded to join often in the Eurcharist, to receive the sacrament of Reconciliation regularly, to read the Scriptures, to pray, and to show your love and care for others.

Then, by living and sharing as an adult Christian, you will be showing everyone who sees you that you have been born again of water and the Spirit.

Questions

1. What are the four steps in the Rite of Christian Initiation for Adults?
2. What are the three sacraments of initiation?
3. What is the process by which you are becoming a member of the Body of Christ? Briefly describe the steps you are taking and the sacraments you have already received.

Activities

1. In a short paragraph, describe a skill you learned or a group you joined in which you used the four steps Nadia used and that are part of Christian initiation. Discuss what you have written.
2. Appoint a committee to study the Rite of Christian Initiation of Adults in detail. Have the committee give a brief chalkboard presentation of what they have discovered.

Renewing Baptism

When you were baptized, either you or your sponsors or your parents made promises to God. You also went through a series of signs, or actions, which were part of the celebration. Take this opportunity as a class to make your baptism new by (1) renewing your baptismal promises and (2) refreshing your memory with some of the outward signs of baptism.

1. *Renewing promises.* Using the outline given below as a guide, write your own personal renewal of what you promised at your baptism. Put all the promises in your own words. Share what you have written with others—in small groups or as a class. At the end, write your own "Amen" for the final statement.

Baptismal Questions	Personal Renewal
1. Do you reject Satan and sin, so as to live in the freedom of God's children? 2. Do you believe in God, the Father almighty, Creator of heaven and earth? 3. Do you believe in Jesus Christ, His only Son, our Lord, who was born of the Virgin Mary, was crucified, died, and was buried, rose from the dead, and is now seated at the right hand of the Father? 4. Do you believe in the Holy Spirit, the holy catholic Church, the Communion of Saints, the forgiveness of sins, the resurrection of the body, and life everlasting?	
This is our faith. This is the faith of the Church. We are proud to profess it, in Christ Jesus our Lord.	

2. *Refreshing the memory.* Review each of the baptismal symbols listed below. Read the short Scripture passage which goes with each symbol. Then, describe one way you can use this symbol

to refresh your memory about your membership
in the Body of Christ.
a. The pouring of water—Romans 6:2–4
b. Anointing with oil—2 Corinthians 1:21–22
c. Receiving a lighted candle—1 John 3:1–2
d. Receiving a white garment—Revelation 3:5

Review

1. Briefly describe what is involved in the process of becoming a member of the Body of Christ.

2. Briefly describe the sacraments of initiation.

3. In your own words, describe the difference between becoming a Christian as a grown-up and becoming a Christian as a young child.

Projects

1. In small groups, write a ceremony for the renewal of baptismal promises. Use the readings and symbols from this chapter. Pages 284–285 of your Handbook will help you with your plans.

2. Make a personal reminder of your own baptism. The reminder can take any form that is practical and useful to you—poster, bookmark, mirror sign, or the like. Share what you have made with your family.

Prayer

God, the Father of our Lord Jesus Christ,
has freed you from all sin,
given you a new birth by water and the Holy Spirit,
and welcomed you into His holy People.
He now anoints you with the oil of salvation.
As Christ was anointed Priest, Prophet, and King,
so may you live always as a member of His Body,
sharing everlasting life.

(Prayer for the anointing after Baptism)

21

Sacraments of Service

In This Chapter

You will review that it is part of membership in the Body of Christ to serve the needs of others.

You will discover that there are many ways for Christians to serve others.

You will find out what the sacrament of Holy Orders means for you.

The Magic Wand

ne of the most popular kinds of story in almost any culture is a tale of sudden magic. Aladdin is given a wonderful lamp containing a genie who will do his bidding. Cinderella discovers a fairy godmother who gives her a pumpkin coach and sends her to a royal dance. An unhappy couple are given three wishes which they waste on petty selfishness. In all of these stories, there is a strange twist of plot. The person who receives this gift of sudden magic always discovers what is really important and valuable in his or her life—usually human love and affection.

Well, right now, you are being given a magic wand—an imaginary one at least. You can do anything you want with your magic wand except use it on yourself. With a copy of the chart below as a guide, describe three human needs. The needs can be worldwide or right next door. Then, briefly explain just what you are going to make happen.

The Human Need	Waving the Wand
1.	
2.	
3.	

Questions

1. Why do you think people are so fascinated by stories of sudden magic?
2. How difficult was it for you to decide what human needs you were going to meet?
3. How did you decide what you were going to do with your magic wand?

Activities

1. Jesus used His abilities and strengths to meet human needs. Select one of the stories of Jesus listed below. Read the story and, in one sentence, write what you feel is the message behind the miracle. Discuss what you have written.
   a. Luke 9:10–17— feeding the hungry
   b. John 17:11–18— healing lepers
   c. Mark 5:25–34— curing the sick
   d. Matthew 9:27–31— restoring sight
   e. John 11:1–44— raising the dead
2. Make a list of needs in your school, parish, or neighborhood. Discuss what is the most important bit of "magic" needed to meet these needs.

Come, Follow Me

esus was standing with Peter, James, and John on the shore of the Sea of Galilee. They had spent the whole day with the crowds and were very tired. Silently, the four of them were watching the last sparkles of sunlight play on the waters. They were jarred out of their silence by a cry from down the beach.

"Rabbi, Rabbi," came the cry from three men trotting along the shoreline. They were dusty from traveling. From the looks of them, they had been walking for some time without rest.

The three came puffing up to Jesus. "Master," one of them gasped, "we are disciples of John the Baptizer. He sent us to see You. He told us to ask You a question."

Jesus put His hand on the man's shoulder. The man took several deep breaths and then continued. "Are You the one who is to come, or should we look for another?"

Jesus let a smile break on His lips as He gave His reply. "Go back and report to John what you hear and see: the blind recover their sight, cripples walk, lepers are cured, and the poor have the Good News preached to them."

The three men looked at one another. They sensed that they had just heard all the answer Jesus was going to give. They knew, too, that the answer was yes—Jesus was the Messiah. But before they could think too long and hard, Jesus took them to the spot on the beach where Philip and Jude had prepared supper. As they ate, Jesus talked about John the Baptizer and asked for news of how he was doing in prison. Chatting by the fire, John's disciples were bursting with happiness. They had met Jesus, and they knew that He was the Messiah.

Sharing the Mission

Wherever Jesus went, He gave out a simple invitation, "Come, follow Me." Jesus was not like the Pied Piper. He did not want troops of people blindly following Him around. Jesus was inviting people to share His mission—to share His ministry. In a way, Jesus was handing on a magic wand. When you were baptized into the Body of Christ, you received that wand, too. That magic wand is the gift of service.

When the disciples of John asked Jesus if He was the Messiah, the Son of God, Jesus did not give them the answer they expected. Jesus did not describe the Father, talk to them about His great power, or give them some sign of His identity. What Jesus told them was, "Look. Recognize that what I am doing is serving others." Because the disciples of John had studied the Scripture, they knew what Isaiah the Prophet had said about the Messiah. When the Messiah comes, Isaiah had said, people would recognize Him by His care for others, especially the poor, the sinners, and the sick.

The time Jesus spent with the disciples was a period of training so that they could share His mission to serve others. Jesus handed on to them the job He had begun. After Pentecost, when thousands of people came to believe in Jesus and to follow Him, each realized that they, too, shared in His mission.

As time went on, the community grew. The followers of Jesus saw the need for special ministries in the Church. The first special ministry that they formed was the office of deacon. The deacons were appointed to take care of the needs of the poor, to see that widows were cared for, and to make sure orphans had homes. But even though the deacons were given a special role, everyone knew that part of being a Christian and being a member of the Body of Christ was a call to serve others.

Some people were called to be teachers, other were called to be healers, and some were called to be administrators. Everyone was called to use his or her talents and gifts in the service of the Body of Christ. There were no free rides in God's kingdom.

Ministry Sacraments

As time went on, the sacraments of service were more clearly defined and celebrated. These sacraments helped people understand and carry out their call to service in the Body of Christ.

1. *Baptism and Confirmation.* By Baptism and by Confirmation, you are given your first call to care for the needs of others. You can respond to that call by living your faith as a lay person. You can also respond to that call by joining a religious order or congregation that performs a special service in the Church.
2. *The order of deacon.* God calls some people to a special ministry of service. These people receive the sacrament of *Holy Orders* and become deacons. The deacons spend their lives teaching, preaching, and caring for the needy.
3. *The order of priest.* God calls some people to another special ministry—to help the bishop, to celebrate the Eucharist, to forgive sins in the sacrament of Reconciliation, to teach, and to help keep the Body of Christ together. Those who receive this call receive the sacrament of Holy Orders and become priests.
4. *The order of bishop.* Because the Body of Christ needs leaders, shepherds, official teachers, and signs of unity, God calls some men to a very special ministry. These men receive Holy Orders and become bishops. The bishops share the same task of service the Apostles had in the early Church. The pope is a bishop and the head of all the bishops.

As important and as special as Holy Orders are, every member of the Body of Christ is a minister. Every member of the Body of Christ shares, in word and action, the Good News of Jesus Christ. Every

Holy Orders One of the seven sacraments of the Church. It is the sacrament of service and leadership for people who want to devote their entire lives to the preaching of the Gospel and to the nourishing of God's Family. The three orders are deacon, priest, and bishop.

member of the Body of Christ is called to reach out to those in need. Every member is asked to be a living Gospel of kindness, patience, unselfishness, honesty, love, faith, and hope.

Just as each of us has one body with many members, and not all the members have the same function, so too we, though many, are one Body in Christ and individually members one of another. We have gifts that differ according to the favor bestowed on each of us.

Your love must be sincere. Detest what is evil, cling to what is good. Love one another with the affection of brothers and sisters. Anticipate one another in showing respect. Do not grow slack but be fervent in spirit; the one you serve is the Lord. Rejoice in hope, be patient under trial, persevere in prayer. Look on the needs of the community as your own; be generous in offering hospitality. Rejoice with those who rejoice, weep with those who weep. Have the same attitude toward all.

(Romans 12:4–6, 9–13, 15–16)

You Are a Minister

What Saint Paul wrote to the Christians in Rome was a kind of guide to ministry in the Body of Christ. In the Gospels and in the Epistles, you can find ways for you to serve in the Body of Christ. Lay people bring Christ to others. They help with youth groups and visit the elderly. They give food and clothing to the poor, and they spend time with someone who is lonely or sad.

Wherever you are and whatever you do, you already are a minister. You may read the Scripture at Mass or serve at the altar. You may help the Saint Vincent de Paul Society. You may *do* all sorts of things. But Christian ministry is not just a job. It is an attitude. The ministry attitude is very simple: "I show how proud and happy I am to be a member of the Body of Christ by helping and serving others."

A Death House in India

The young sister stood outside the room quivering in fright. She knew what she was called to do, but this was her first day in the hospice. She peeked into the room and saw row after row of cots. She saw the people lying on those cots. They were dying. She saw the other sisters moving quickly from cot to cot—pouring water here, giving a kind word there, touching hands, and giving medicine.

Behind her, the young sister heard the familiar *flip-flop* of Mother Teresa's sandals. Quickly, she wiped away the tears that had started to trickle down her cheeks. In a moment, Mother Teresa had her by the arm.

"Sister Anna," Mother Teresa said kindly, "this is your first day here?"

"Yes, Mother," the sister replied.

"Good, good," said the wrinkled lady with the heavenly smile. "Come with me. I have someone I want you to meet."

Mother Teresa took Sister Anna by the hand and led her down one of the aisles between the cots. Soon, they arrived at a cot in the far corner of the huge room. On the cot lay a human skeleton. His eyes were sunk deep into his head. His hair was gone. He had only one tooth in his mouth. His hands trembled as he reached out to Mother Teresa.

The nun took the man's face in her large gentle hands. With her head, she motioned for Sister Anna to kneel down beside her. "Sister Anna," Mother Teresa said, "I'd like you to meet Jesus."

Questions

1. What was Jesus' answer to the disciples?
2. What are the sacraments of ministry? Explain what each one means.
3. What is the lesson of the story of Mother Teresa and Sister Anna?
4. In what ways can you share the gift of ministry with others?

Activities

1. In small groups, make a list of five attitudes you think people need when they are ministering to the needs of others. Make sure everyone agrees on each attitude. Rank the attitudes in order of importance. When the group has finished, share your work with the whole class. Vote for what the class thinks are the top five attitudes of those mentioned.

2. Select one of the passages listed below. Read the passage carefully and then write a personal resolution on how you can minister to the needs of others.
   a. Matthew 13:4–53
   b. Mark 4:1–41
   c. Luke 5:17–49

Training for Ministry

omeday, you may feel a call to become a member of a religious order as a sister or brother. Someday, you might be called to be a deacon or priest. But right now, you are a young minister in the Body of Christ. By serving, you are learning ways that you can care for other members of the Church and people who need you.

Carefully read the instruction on page 232. It is adapted from the actual words the bishop uses when he is welcoming candidates into the final stages of preparation for ordination as deacons and priests. Long ago, this used to be called the rite of *Tonsure*. Today, it is called the Admission to Candidacy for Ordination. For each number in the

Tonsure The ancient ceremony by which a person became a member of the clergy. During tonsure, a lock of hair was cut from the crown of a person's head. The word *tonsure* means "haircut."

instruction, answer the following three questions: (1) What am I doing about this now? (2) How can I prepare myself to do more? and (3) How can I help others do more? Then, write your own answer to the question at the end.

Call to Training for Christian Ministers

Our brothers and sisters are here today in the presence of the Church. They want to be ministers in the Body of Christ. Jesus gave this command: "Ask the Lord of the harvest to send laborers into His harvest." Our brothers and sisters here are asked by their baptisms to help with the harvest. We now see if they are ready for their training. Here are some of the signs of people ready to share ministry in the Body of Christ.

1. They are willing to answer God and the community with the words of the prophet, "Here I am, Lord. Send me."
2. They see and are aware of the needs of others.
3. They receive the sacraments regularly.
4. They spend time in prayer and in studying the Gospels.
5. They practice serving others.

Brothers and sisters, are you ready to prepare yourselves in mind and heart to give faithful service to Christ the Lord and His Body, the Church?

Review

Circle the T if the statement is true. Circle the F if the statement is false.

1. The disciples of John did not understand the answer Jesus gave them.   T   F

2. Only a chosen few have the gift of ministry.   T   F

3. The order of deacon is part of the sacrament of Reconciliation.   T   F

4. Bishops receive the sacrament of Holy Orders to help them teach and lead in the Body of Christ.   T   F

5. It is important to be aware of others' needs when you prepare yourself for service.   T   F

Projects

1. In small groups or as a class, decide on needed ministries in your parish which you can perform. Make sure that you are realistic in what you list. You may want to investigate parish groups, other classes, the parish team, and the like. Then, plan a special service project for your class.

2. Have a special "Vocations Day" celebration. Appoint committees to study the priesthood, the diaconate, the religious life, and the various lay ministries that are possible. Have special reports, prayer services, and displays for your vocations celebration.

Prayer

Let us ask our God and Lord to pour out His grace and blessing on people who desire to give their whole lives to ministry. Let them draw closer to Christ and be His witnesses in the world. May they share the burdens of others and always listen to the voice of the Holy Spirit. May they strengthen the faith of their brothers and sisters by their word and example. This we ask through Christ our Lord. Amen.

(A prayer for vocations)

22

Sacraments of Healing

In This Chapter

You will discover that the followers of Jesus have a healing attitude.

You will learn more about the sacraments of healing.

You will see how you can have a healing attitude.

The Doorkeeper

Father Solanus shuffled down the whitewashed inner court of Saint Bonaventure's Monastery in Detroit, Michigan. He looked out the windows as he walked. A robin was pecking for worms on the grass of the tiny yard. The bearded old man made a right turn and headed for the door which led to the parlor. His world was very small. His job was very simple. He whispered a little prayer to the Blessed Mother as he began his day's work—the same work he had done for almost fifty years.

He went to the monastery entrance and threw back the bolt. He heard the honking and squealing that told of auto workers racing down Mount Elliott Avenue on their way to the factory. Already in the early morning, there was a huge line of people along the red brick front of the monastery. Over one hundred people were waiting for him. All were in need. Some needed food or clothing. Most of them needed God's healing.

One by one, the people came to Father Solanus, kissed his hand, and asked for his blessing. Everyone had a request. "My husband is out of a job. Help him, Father," said one. "I have cancer, Father Solanus. Please pray for me," said another. "My daughter is blind. Can you do something, Father?"

For each one, the priest had a few kind words. Then, he would send the people through the passage that led to the church. He would urge them to receive the sacrament of Reconciliation and to stay for Mass. Many of the people had their requests answered.

All of a sudden, a young mother with tears running down her cheeks came before Father Solanus. She was holding a baby not yet a year old. "Thank you for healing my baby, Father," she said. "The doctor did not think she would live a week..."

A flash of Irish temper glittered in Father Solanus's eyes. "I did not heal your baby," he said. "The love of God and the power of His Word and the sacraments healed her."

Father Solanus Casey was born in a small village in northern Wisconsin. When he was a young man, he tried to become a lumberjack, but he was not strong enough. When he was in his early twenties, he moved to Detroit. He was attracted to religious life and joined the *Capuchins*. After Solanus was ordained to the priesthood, he failed his final examinations. As a result, he was never allowed to hear confessions or to preach in public. He was given the job of doorkeeper at the monastery.

Before very long, the people in Detroit sensed the great faith and love of Father Solanus. They soon realized that this simple man was very, very close to God and to the Blessed Mother. They also saw that the doorkeeper of Saint Bonaventure's brought the gift of healing to the people he met at the door. Thousands of people confessed their sins and returned to the Church. Hundreds told stories of being healed of sicknesses and injuries.

Father Solanus died in 1957. The whole city of Detroit was sad. They wanted Father Solanus to be made a saint of the Church. Even though he may never be made an official saint, Father Solanus has a place in the people's memories. Those who were touched by the kindness and love of the doorkeeper of Saint Bonaventure's will always remember his healing love and his faith in the healing power of the sacraments.

Capuchins   A branch of the Franciscan order. The Capuchins were founded by Brother Matthew of Urbano in 1525. Their name comes from the pointed hood, or capuche, worn by members of the order.

Questions

1. What kind of person do you think Father Solanus was?
2. How did he bring the healing love of Jesus to the people of Detroit?
3. How do you feel when you are sick?

Activities

1. Select one of the two readings listed below. After you have carefully studied the reading, write in your own words the healing attitude you found there.
   a. 2 Corinthians 4:16—18
   b. Colossians 1:24

2. Appoint a committee to find out what your parish does for its sick members. After the committee has made its report to the class, discuss how the member of your class can help.

Forgiveness and Health

Ed lost his balance for just a split second. The skateboard darted into the street. Then, everything seemed to happen at once. Ed saw the red car, heard the brakes, and felt the impact of the car. He also felt the shooting pain in his leg.

Before he knew it, he was lying in the street. He heard footsteps. He saw a woman looking in his eyes. "He's alive!" she said. "But he has a compound fracture of his leg." That was the last thing Ed remembered. He fainted.

When Ed woke up, he was in a hospital bed. He had a huge cast on his leg. A doctor was writing something on a clipboard. "That was a close call, young man," the doctor said. She put her hand on Ed's forehead to see whether or not he was feverish.

"Did you fix my leg?" Ed asked.

The doctor smiled and explained, "Broken legs don't get fixed, Ed. They heal. What I did was clean and purify your wound. Then, I put the leg back in place. The cast will keep it that way. Now, you have to have patience and give the leg time to heal."

God's Healing

When Jesus was on earth, He spent much of His public life offering people a chance to heal. Everybody goes through some kind of suffering—illness, sinfulness, injury, loss, or the like. The ministry of Jesus pointed out how important it is for members of the Body of Christ to have healing attitudes. The Church sees three very special signs of healing in the community—three sacraments which celebrate healing in the lives of members.

The followers of Jesus experience healing and peace when they receive Holy Communion. They know that celebrating the Eucharist and receiving the Body and Blood of Jesus help them turn away from wrong choices and give them inner peace. They also experience healing from their sins in the sacrament of Reconciliation. There, they receive absolution for their sins and feel like part of the Body of Christ again. They also experience healing in the Anointing of the Sick. The members of the Body who are seriously ill have the peace and love of the community to help them recover from their illness and to experience the peace of Christ in their suffering.

In these sacraments, the same healing steps the doctor explained to Ed take place in the hearts and the bodies of the faithful. The chart below will help you see those steps in action for the healing sacraments.

Step One: Cleanse and purify the wound.

a. *Eucharist.* At the beginning of Mass, people acknowledge their sins.

b. *Reconciliation.* People acknowledge their need for healing and forgiveness. They face their sinfulness and express their sorrow.

c. *Anointing.* The person who is seriously ill comes to the community. The priest and people share the Word of God and pray for the person.

Step Two: Put the wounded part back in the right place.

a. *Eucharist.* The people share the sign of peace and the Body of Christ.

b. *Reconciliation.* The people share the Scriptures, confess their sins, accept a penance, and receive absolution from the priest.

c. *Anointing.* The sick person joins in the prayer and is anointed with oil.

Step Three: Provide patience, time, and rest to let healing happen.

a. *Eucharist.* The people leave the Mass and try to do better.

b. *Reconciliation.* The people do the penance they have been given. They try to avoid sin and to be faithful members of the Body.

c. *Anointing.* The sick person trusts in the healing power of God's Word and sacrament. He or she tries to accept whatever God has planned.

These three steps are very important healing attitudes because healing is not fixing. Healing takes time. Some people are afraid to go to doctors. They are afraid to find out they are sick. But the followers of Jesus know that they are always in need of healing. And you have to know that you need healing before the healing process can begin.

Christians Are Healers

For a certain period of time in the Church, people were very shy about receiving the sacraments. For several hundred years, most people thought they were not worthy to receive such wonderful gifts. People rarely went to Communion. They went to confession only when they really had to. They received Anointing at the last possible moment. The sacrament was even called Extreme Unction, or Last Anointing. But in the twentieth century, there has been a rebirth of the sacraments. People are again seeing how important these signs are for the life of the Body of Christ.

Christians also carry their healing attitudes away from the sacraments. As the followers of Jesus reach out to one another, they want to cleanse and to purify the wounds that are keeping them from being kind, caring, and unselfish people. Parents and children work together to put their relationships back in the right place. Friends and neighbors are patient with one another and are spending time with one another to let their relationships grow.

When you make these healing attitudes your own and when you receive the sacraments of healing, you can see why the ministry of healing is such an important part of following Jesus. Jesus saw sickness and sin as signs that something was wrong inside people. Because Jesus loved people so much, He wanted to make things right. Christian love is a "make things right" kind of love. It is a healing love.

Suffering Has Meaning

Marian Armstrong had cancer. The doctors said her condition was very serious. She had come to a special Mass at Saint Raphael's parish. At Mass, the people of the parish who were seriously ill or very old received the sacrament of the Anointing of the Sick. Mrs. Armstrong listened to the reading from Saint James:

Is there anyone sick among you? This person should ask for the priests of the Church. They in turn are to pray over this person, anointing him or her with oil in the Name of the Lord. This prayer uttered in faith will reclaim the one who is ill, and the Lord will restore this person to health. If this person has committed any sins, forgiveness will be his or hers.

(James 5:14–15)

The priest anointed each sick person on the head and on the hands. Everyone prayed and sang together. Finally, everyone received Holy Communion. Marian Armstrong went home to her family feeling happy and at peace.

In the days and weeks that followed, Mrs. Armstrong did not get better. Her cancer got worse. But she seemed very, very peaceful inside. She talked about her illness with her husband and children. She shared the feelings she was having inside. One day, a Eucharistic minister from the parish brought Communion to Mrs. Armstrong in her bedroom. Her husband and children received Communion, too. The Eucharistic minister explained that the Communion was food for her journey. He called it *Viaticum*. Late that same evening, Mrs. Armstrong died.

Through her tears, one of Marian Armstrong's daughters said, "I thought she would be healed. I thought that when she was anointed, she would be healed."

Her father hugged her close. "Even though your mother's cancer was not cured," he said, "she was really healed. And it is time for the suffering to end. It is time for her to be happy with Jesus—forever."

Viaticum The sacrament of the dying. When a person is dying, he or she is given the sacrament of Holy Communion, and special prayers are said. The word *viaticum* means "food for the journey."

Questions

1. What are the three steps in the process of healing?
2. How is each of the following a sacrament of healing—the Eucharist, Reconciliation, Anointing?
3. In what ways are members of the Body of Christ healers?
4. How can you be a healer in the way you think and act?

Activities

1. Before receiving the sacrament of Reconciliation, it is a custom to look at your life and to see what wrong choices you have made—what sins you have committed. Write five questions you could ask yourself to help you discover your need for healing before receiving the sacrament.
2. In small groups, discuss the story of the crippled man (Luke 5:17–26). What does this story tell about the forgiveness of sins? What does this story tell about healing?

Learning Healing Attitudes

In order to use the sacraments of healing well and to fulfill your own ministry of healing, it is very important for you to grow in your healing attitudes. Carefully completing the following exercise can help you grow in those attitudes.

Using the diagram below as a guide, describe how you already have each attitude listed. Then, make one plan for growing in the attitude. Finally, also make one plan for helping others have the healing attitude. When you have finished, discuss with the class what you have done. After the discussion, privately decide on one area in your life where you need healing. Briefly pray about how you can seek the healing you need.

Attitude	How I Have It	How I Will Grow	How I Will Share
Aware of the need for healing			
Cleanse and purify			
Put things back in place			
Have patience and provide time			

Review

Fill in the missing words.

1. Father Solanus had a special gift of ___.

2. The ministry of Jesus pointed out how important it is for members of the Body of Christ to have healing ___.

3. For healing to begin, it is important to ___ and to purify the wound.

4. In the sacrament of Reconciliation, people ___ their sins to a priest.

5. Being healed is not necessarily the same as being ___ of a disease.

Projects

1. Plan a special prayer service of healing. Include in your prayer service the healing attitudes you have learned in the chapter. Choose readings used in this chapter. Select some music from your parish hymnal. The music should show healing attitudes. Pages 284–285 of your Handbook will help you with your plans.

2. Make a "Christian Healing" bulletin-board display or poster. On the display, show how your parish shares the healing attitudes. Also show how your parish celebrates the sacraments of healing.

3. Have a family discussion on the need for healing. Share the attitudes you have learned with your family. Together make a family pledge to help one another have attitudes of healing in the home.

Prayer

Lord Jesus Christ, our Redeemer,
by the power of the Holy Spirit,
ease the sufferings of our sick brothers and sisters.
Make them well again in mind and body.
In Your loving kindness, forgive their sins
and grant them full health
so that they may be restored to Your service.
You are Lord for ever and ever.

(Prayer for the sacrament of Anointing)

23

Sacraments of Family

In This Chapter

You will review the importance of the family in the Body of Christ.

You will see how the sacraments of Marriage and Eucharist help families follow Jesus.

You will discover ways in which you can develop good family attitudes.

What Is a Family?

efore you ever thought about being a follower of Jesus, you were a member of a family. Maybe your family is a big and noisy group with brothers, sisters, parents, grandparents, aunts, uncles, and cousins. Maybe your family is tiny— just you and your mother or you and your father. Perhaps you were born into your family, or maybe you were adopted into yours. But no matter what your family looks like or how you got there, your family taught you and continues to teach you who you are.

Using the outline below as a guide, write some information about your family. Feel free to share or not to share what you have written. When you have finished, in your own words, answer this question: "What is a family?"

1. Briefly describe your family. Who belongs to it?
2. List three things your family gives to you.
3. List three things you give to your family.
4. List three things that you know or do today that you first learned at home.
5. Describe one thing about your family that you hope never changes.
6. Describe one thing about your family that you would like to change.
7. In ten words or less, tell who you are.

Questions

1. Which of the seven items in the outline was the easiest for you to answer? the hardest?
2. In what you wrote, what word occurred most frequently? Why?
3. Did you ever feel like running away from home? Why or why not?

Activities

1. Discuss everybody's individual definition of a family. Put all the differences on the board. Then, as a class, make a definition of *family* which everyone can agree on. Share that definition with your own family.

2. In small groups, choose one of the passages listed below. Read the passage in the group. Then, talk about what this reading from God's Word has to do with families.
   a. Ephesians 6:1–4
   b. 1 Peter 4:8–11
   c. 1 John 4:7–9

A Love Story

hen the astronauts first saw the earth from outer space, the planet looked to them like a huge blue marble. They could hardly believe that this beautiful glowing sphere contained over four billion people. Down on the planet, each one of those over four billion people has a story to tell. Each of those people has a family.

Over four thousand years ago, God reached down to a tiny pin prick on the blue marble. There He found two people in love—Abraham and Sarah. Even though these two people were very old and past their childbearing years, God told them that they were going to be the beginning of a new and extremely large family—the People of God.

The had a son named Isaac. Through that son, the love and faith of Abraham and Sarah was passed on to family after family. The *twelve tribes* of Israel remembered the faith of Abraham and Sarah. In every family, the love of God was celebrated, and His great deeds were told again and again.

When Jesus was born, He was a part of the family of Abraham and Sarah—the People of God. He heard Mary and Joseph handing on the stories and truths of the Jewish faith. In His little family, He learned about His Father, He was nourished and fed, He prayed, and He saw many examples of love and kindness.

After Jesus rose from the dead, and the Church began to spread throughout the world, young people first heard about the story of Jesus from their mothers and fathers. It was in the love of the family that the flame of faith was lighted and kept burning. In the family, young people learned how to pray and how to love. In the family, the love of the husband and wife was a reminder of just how much Jesus loves His People.

Twelve tribes The twelve divisions in the kingdom of Israel. Each of the twelve tribes was named for one of Jacob's sons. Another name for Jacob was Israel.

A Special Sacrament

From the very beginning of the Church, marriage was a sacrament—an outward sign of some invisible grace. When a believing woman and a believing man promised to love each other forever, Jesus was there. For the first few centuries after the resurrection, however, there was no special Church wedding. Christians followed the marriage laws and ceremonies of the country in which they lived. The very fact that two believing people came together in marriage was enough to show that the sacrament had taken place. Besides, the sacrament was not contained in the ceremony. The sacrament was in the day-to-day love of the husband and wife and their children.

But the whole community had a part in this love, too. So, it was the custom for the friends and families of the couple to come together to welcome the bride and groom into a new way of living—into a new little family. There was always a party because this was a happy sacrament of shared love. Often, the local priest or bishop was invited to the party. During the feast, the bishop or priest would say a prayer asking God in the name of the whole believing community to bless the bride and groom. Today, it is a law of the Church that Catholic couples should have their marriage witnessed by a priest.

The marriage celebration is a reminder that the love between a man and a woman is a good and holy thing. The physical and emotional closeness they share is not only part of God's plan for them, but it is also the way they are meant to follow Jesus. This sharing does not stop at the wedding. Instead, it can grow better and better. Marriage is an everyday sacrament. Marriage is also a sacrament that is shared with the children, too. One of the purposes of marriage is to have and to care for children. Another purpose of marriage is to grow closer and closer in love—to fight loneliness and fear. The two purposes make sure that the marriage binds people together in a loving family.

Family Attitudes

Marriage and family life are made up of millions of little things. There is work to do every day. There are tears to be wiped as well as beds to be made. There are hands to be held as well as meals to be prepared. In a family, husband, wife, and children share everything—happiness, sorrow, work, play, good times, and bad times.

In the wedding ceremony, little seeds are planted in the lives of the two people who love each other. These seeds are the attitudes and skills that are needed in any family. These attitudes and skills are also needed by the children who grow up in the family. The chart below shows some of the attitudes and skills that are mentioned in the Rite of Marriage. There is also a very brief description of each.

Attitudes	Skills
1. *Love.* Really having an honest sense of care and concern.	1. *Support.* The ability to look out for one another and care for one another.
2. *Honor.* Always seeing the good in the members of the family.	2. *Forgiveness.* The ability to give one another a new start.
3. *Respect.* Always seeing one another as individuals with strengths and weaknesses.	3. *Cooperation.* The ability to give and to take when doing what needs to be done in the family.
4. *Loyalty.* Feeling a sense of belonging.	4. *Faithfulness.* The ability to stick together.

The Holy Spirit is with each family to help the members grow in these family attitudes and skills. When people see a family growing in these attitudes and skills, they can see a little better how much Jesus loves His People.

Wounded Families

No marriage is perfect. You see, a family is not a painting or a statue. A family is alive. As with every living thing, there are hurts and wounds. Some hurts and wounds are little, like quarreling, forgetfulness, scolding, or misunderstanding. These hurts heal easily. But there are other hurts in marriages and families that are much deeper, and sometimes families come apart.

At every wedding ceremony, the man and the woman promise to be together forever. If the two people really try and depend on God for help, if they really love and care always, they will be together till death. Sometimes, a husband and wife separate or even get a divorce. Divorce is a deep wound in a family. It hurts the husband and the wife, and if there are children, the divorce hurts them very much, too.

Even though a divorce deeply hurts and wounds a family, divorce does not destroy a family. In families where the husband and wife are apart, each must show special love and respect for the children, so that everyone can pick up the pieces, seek God's forgiveness, and make the best of a very hurtful situation.

Whenever there is a wound in a family, it is very important not to be hard judges. God sees into people's hearts. He understands what has gone wrong. His Spirit is with the family to help them change and grow.

The same is true for the other wounds in a family—alcoholism, serious fighting, runaways, and so on. But it is also very important for wounded families to get help from others. The same community that was happy and feasted at the wedding is also part of a support group for married couples and families. The community as a whole can see that families get the help they need.

Family Meals

Mealtime can be a very important time for families. At meals, there is a chance to share what has been happening during the day. At meals, parents and children can share what is really important in their thoughts and feelings. Meals are times for laughter and stories, too. Not only do families need to feed the body, families also need to feed and to strengthen their family attitudes and skills.

For that reason, there is another very important meal in the life of every Catholic family—the Eucharist. When a family comes together to share the Eucharist, they see how important each member is. They share their faith and give one another moral support. So, the Eucharist is another very important family sacrament. Together at the Table of the Lord, the family can ask God to be with them and to help them love, honor, respect, and be loyal to one another.

And the family can bring those prayers home, too. Families can take a few seconds every day to share prayer—especially before and after meals. By pray-

ing together, families remember that God is a very important ingredient that can help make their families work.

Do What He Tells You

The chief steward was pulling his hair out by the roots. He didn't know how he could have made such a terrible mistake. The bride and groom were so happy. The house was decorated so perfectly. The food was excellent. But they were about to run out of wine.

Mary noticed what was happening. Quickly, she went to Jesus. "They have no more wine," she said to Jesus—simply and clearly.

"What would you want Me to do?" Jesus asked.

Mary just smiled at her Son. Then, she went and spoke to the people who were serving at the tables. "Do whatever He tells you," she said to them.

Jesus asked the waiters to fill six stone jars with water. He told them to take some to the steward. What a miracle! The water had become wine.

Remember to pray to the Blessed Mother in your family. She has a special love and care for Christian families. Let her know your needs. She will certainly tell her Son about them. The words Mary spoke at the wedding feast can help you grow in your family attitudes and skills: "Do whatever He tells you."

Questions

1. What is the importance of the sacrament of Marriage?
2. What is the purpose of the wedding ceremony?
3. What are two purposes of marriage?
4. What are some wounds that families experience? How can these wounds be healed?
5. How can the Eucharistic Meal help you be a better family member?

Activities

1. Appoint a committee to study how the sacrament of Marriage is celebrated in your parish. What preparation does the couple have to make? What are some parish wedding customs? What are the words used at the wedding ceremony? Have the committee report to the class and then discuss the report.
2. Write one question about the sacrament of Marriage on a small slip of paper. Collect all the papers and pick the top five questions. Then, your teacher or some other resource person can help you arrive at the answers.

Getting Ready

Christian marriage is a vocation. That means that marriage is a way that many people use to be good and faithful members of the Body of Christ. You do not have any way of knowing right now whether or not you will be married. But you are and always will be a member of a family. Being a good family member means you have a responsibility to grow in family attitudes and skills—to become the best *you* that you can possibly be. Using the chart below as a guide, describe one way in which you can develop each attitude or skill right now. Then, describe how you can help one another develop these attitudes and skills. Discuss the results in class.

Attitudes and Skills	Way to Develop	Way to Help
1. Love		
2. Support		
3. Honor		
4. Forgiveness		
5. Respect		
6. Cooperation		
7. Loyalty		
8. Faithfulness		

Review

Complete the following statements in your own words.

1. Marriage is a sacrament because ...

2. Two family attitudes are ...

3. Two family skills are . . .

4. No marriage is perfect because . . .

5. Mealtime is important in a family because . . .

6. The Eucharist is important for families because . . .

Projects

1. As an exercise for your imagination, project yourself forward in history five hundred years. The idea of family has been lost. It is your task to rebuild the family unit from scratch. Write out a plan for restoring the family unit. Include in your plan some of the ideas you have learned in this chapter.

2. If possible, invite a Marriage Encounter couple to your class. Ask this couple to share with you the ways families can support one another. Ask them to explain what Marriage Encounter is.

3. Share the attitudes and skills you learned about in this chapter with your own family. At a family meal, discuss how you can help one another in the family develop these attitudes and skills.

Prayer

Father, stretch out Your hand, and bless all married couples—all families. Lord, grant that as they live the sacrament of marriage, they share with one another the gifts of Your love. Let husbands and wives become one in heart and mind as witnesses to Your presence in their marriages. Help each couple create a home together. Father, grant that as they come together to Your Table on earth, so may they one day have the joy of sharing Your feast in heaven.

(Adapted from the wedding blessing)

24

Pray Always

In This Chapter

You will review the great importance of prayer for you as a follower of Jesus.

You will learn the different ways members of the Body of Christ pray.

You will discover how you can pray always.

Talking with a Friend

The noise in the school yard was deafening. Father John stepped into the sunlight to watch the games. The younger boys were playing tag near the laundry room. The middle-grade boys raced around the edge of the yard in a complicated version of hide and seek. In the center of the yard, the older boys kicked up the dust in a hearty game of football.

Father John loved to watch the boys of the Oratory at their games. Not so many years ago, boys like this in Turin, Italy, would be putting their energy into troublemaking—stealing, fighting, and vandalizing. But now, these boys had a place to call their own, and their energy could be put into learning, playing, and praying.

The priest's eyes settled on a frail-looking boy in the center of the football game. "Ah, Dominic," Don Bosco whispered to himself, "you look half-dead out there. Where do you get your strength?"

"Hey, Luigi," shouted Dominic, "pass the ball to me—quick, quick!"

Dominic missed the pass, but Pasquale came up behind Dominic. He saved the pass and, with some nimble footwork, kicked in a goal. The first one to congratulate Pasquale was Dominic.

Just then, the small bell in the campanile signaled the end of playtime. Boys of all ages and sizes dashed off in different directions. It was time for chores.

Don Bosco walked slowly across the school yard. "Well, Lord," the priest prayed, "it seems as though Your work is being done here at the Oratory. But I am very worried about Dominic Savio. He is such a good and energetic boy. He is so very close to You and Your Blessed Mother. But his health is not good. Take care of him, Lord."

Just then, Father John saw Dominic, with a broom, entering the classroom building. The priest followed him into the building. John watched as Dominic began his work. After a few moments, Don Bosco walked up to Dominic. The boy did not seem to notice the priest. Dominic's lips were moving, but no sound came out.

"Dominic!" said the priest. No answer. "Dominic!" he said again—louder this time.

The boy looked up. He seemed surprised to see Don Bosco standing in front of him. "Oh, Father," Dominic said, "I am sorry. I was just talking with my Friend. It won't be long now, you know."

A puzzled look crept across Don Bosco's face. "What do you mean, Dominic?" the priest said.

"I am going home soon," said the boy.

Six months later, Dominic Savio was dead. He was just fifteen years old. Now, both Saint John Bosco and Saint Dominic Savio have all the time they want for talking with their Friend.

Questions

1. From this story, what kind of person do you think John Bosco was? Dominic Savio?
2. Why was Don Bosco so concerned about Dominic?
3. What are some of the ways you talk to your friends? Do you ever talk to God that way?

Activities

1. Make a list of the times in the last twenty-four hours that you talked to a friend. Pick one of the times listed and describe what you talked about. Share with the class what you have written. What are the topics friends talk about most frequently?
2. Read what Jesus told His Apostles about praying (Matthew 6:5–13). In small groups, discuss the lesson Jesus was giving the Apostles. What can you learn about praying from these words of Jesus?

Never at a Loss for Words

Beth Ann walked slowly across the porch. She felt just a little embarrassed. What if Mrs. Tompitch laughed at her? If that happened, she would just die. Beth Ann had overheard her father and Deacon McDonald talking about Mrs. Tompitch. They were saying that she was a woman of "great prayer." Well, Beth Ann wanted to learn more about prayer, so who better to talk to? Finally, the girl bit her lower lip, closed her eyes, and rang the doorbell.

In a moment, the door opened. "Hi there," said Mrs. Tompitch. "What can I do for you, young lady?"

Mrs. Tompitch looked very ordinary. Beth Ann almost expected her to glow or something. "My name is Beth Ann," she blurted out, "and I heard from my father and the parish deacon that you know a lot about praying. And I wanted to know more, too. So, I thought I'd ask you about it. And I hope that I can learn something. And—and—and is this all sounding pretty stupid?"

Mrs. Tompitch just laughed. "Come on in, Beth Ann," she said. "It doesn't sound stupid at all."

Five minutes later, Beth Ann and Mrs. Tompitch were sitting at the kitchen table, eating bran muffins and drinking hot tea. "I'm flattered that your father and the deacon both think I know a lot about prayer. But I have been praying so long, I don't think about the 'hows' too much anymore."

Beth Ann took another bite of her muffin and patiently waited to hear more.

"Who are you?" Mrs. Tompitch asked.

"Beth Ann Taylor," the girl replied.

"Tell me more about who you are," Mrs. Tompitch urged.

"Well," the girl continued, "I live in an apartment on Ridgeway Avenue. I have a little brother and a canary. I go to King Junior High. I am a member of Saint Paul's parish. I go to religion class on Thursday afternoons. I am taking guitar lessons. And then, I want to be ..."

Mrs. Tompitch interrupted. "And when you chat with your family and friends, what do you talk about?"

"All those things," Beth Ann replied.

"You have just learned lesson number one about prayer," Mrs. Tompitch said, with a grin. "I used to think praying—serious praying—was just for nuns and priests. Then, I realized that prayer is just a fancy word for communicating with God. I am pretty good at communicating with people, so I thought I just might be good at talking to God."

"That sounds too easy," Beth Ann said.

"Oh, sometimes it is easy. Sometimes it is hard," said Mrs. Tompitch. "But prayer is always just communicating with God the Father, your Brother Jesus, your Friend the Holy Spirit, your Mother Mary, the angels, or the saints. Would you like another muffin?"

Ways to Pray

Throughout your years as a member of the Body of Christ, you have learned many different ways to pray. You have learned how to pray to God in your own words. You have learned how the group can pray together in prayer services, the Eucharistic Celebration, and the sacraments. You have learned that just being quiet and listening to God is a way to pray, too. You have learned that reading the Bible, God's inspired Word, is another way to pray.

All through your life, you will be learning more and more about communicating with people. The more you learn about communicating with people, the more you learn about praying. When you see an old married couple sitting hand in hand on a park bench, you learn that prayer can be sitting quietly with somebody you love—not saying a word. When you learn the rules of order for official meetings and school assemblies, you are learning how to make formal prayer more real, too.

When you learn how friends often use the same words over and over, tell the same stories, and relive the same experiences, you can see the importance of learning some prayers by heart. Remember that prayer is communicating with God, and communication is a two-way street. It involves listening as well as talking. So, when you realize that you have to listen in science class in order to get the lesson, you know that you have to listen to God, too. You can listen to Him in church, in religion class, in the words of your parents, in the words of a friend, and in the quiet of your own heart.

Kinds of Prayer

There are as many kinds of prayer as there are kinds of conversation. What you talk to people about are the same kinds of things you can talk to God about. The chart below will help you see how snatches from real human conversation are made up of the same elements as the traditional kinds of prayer.

Contrition Sorrow for one's sins. Catholics say a prayer of contrition during the celebration of the sacrament of Reconciliation.

Snatches of Conversation	Kinds of Prayer
1. "Gee, you look just great today!"	Praise
2. "Karen, please give me a hand with my homework."	Petition, or asking
3. "Oh, Uncle Frank, thank you so much for the new football."	Thanksgiving
4. "Mr. Schultz, I am very sorry I broke your window."	Sorrow or *contrition*
5. "Kelly, you will never guess what happened to me today."	Information or simple conversation

Something to Talk About

As you went through this book, you learned more and more about what it means to be a follower of Jesus Christ. You discovered again that you are somebody very, very special. You are loved by God your Father, you have been forgiven, and you will live forever. You have discovered more and more about Jesus, His message, and His love.

Besides that, you have seen how to act as a member of the Body of Christ. You learned that a follower of Jesus Christ has a love that is peaceful, patient, kind, unselfish, and honest. You have learned, too, that the Mass and the sacraments help you remember that you are part of the Body of Christ. For a wonderful person like you, prayer is not meant to be a chore—it is the frosting on the cake.

Prayer is the way you and your fellow members of the Body of Christ keep in contact with your Friend. It is the way you grow as a follower of Jesus. It is the way you share everything you are and everything you will become with those who love you very, very much—the Father, Jesus, the Spirit, Mary, and the saints. You are an honored daughter or son in a very wonderful Family. Prayer is your right, your privilege, and your duty as a member of the Family.

Remember, too, that prayer is not a sign of weakness. It is a source of strength. On Calvary, Dismas was dying. He knew he was a criminal. He knew very well all the serious crimes he had committed. But Dismas was puzzled about the man who was nailed to the cross next to him. Everybody was taunting the man so. Yet, this person did not look like a criminal. After a time, Dismas looked toward Jesus and said a very short, very simple prayer. But that prayer has been remembered by every person who has ever followed Jesus Christ.

"Jesus," said Dismas, "remember me when You enter Your kingdom."

Jesus looked at Dismas and replied, "I assure you. Today, you will be with Me in paradise."

Questions

1. What is prayer?
2. What are some of the ways to pray? What are some of the kinds of prayer?
3. What is one of the best ways to learn more about praying?
4. What is your favorite kind of prayer? Why is it your favorite?

Activities

1. Write down in a notebook some of the ways you talk to others during a single day. For each item of conversation you write about, write how that item can teach you about prayer.

2. Study the chart on the kinds of prayer. In small groups, discuss the kind of prayer each person uses most often. Why do you think this is so? How can you help one another to use all the kinds of prayer?

Learning to Pray Always

Praying, like good conversation, takes practice. An old monk, when asked about prayer, said he was going to write a book about prayer. "The book will have three chapters," said the monk. "The first chapter will read: 'Pray!' The second chapter will read: 'Pray some more!' The third chapter will read: 'Keep on praying!'"

Make a copy of the chart below. Across the top are printed the kinds of prayer. Along the left side are printed some of the ways to pray. Working alone at first, try to fill in each square with an example of how you can use each kind of prayer in each way. After you have spent some time working alone, share in small groups what you have done. Work until everyone has filled in every square. Discuss what you have written.

Ways	Praise	Thanksgiving	Petition	Sorrow	Conversation
1. Alone					
2. Without words					
3. At Mass					
4. Memorized prayer					
5. Listening					

Review

1. What is the lesson in the story of Saint John Bosco and Saint Dominic Savio?

2. What is prayer?

3. List three ways to pray.

4. List three kinds of prayer and explain each.

5. What was the prayer of Saint Dismas?

Projects

1. Many saints and holy people have been mentioned in this book. Go through the book and make a list of these people. Then, prepare your own Litany of the Saints. For each person mentioned, write one quality you can learn from him or her. Then, choose a response to say. For example: "Saint Joseph, you taught us how to be unselfish in our love. Pray for us." Pray the litany in class. Share the litany with your family.

2. Set up a summer support system. Get a partner for the summer. (Maybe three or four could work together.) Plan ways to continue growing in your membership in the Body of Christ. Include three parts in your plans: (a) Bible reading, (b) reaching out to others, and (c) prayer and worship. Be creative in your plans but be practical, too.

Prayer

Christ lived here among us,
He worked here among us,
Morning, night, and day.
Showed us His glory,
gave us a promise,
and even though we turned away:
Christ is our Lord and our King.

Oh, what a gift, what a wonderful gift;
who can tell the wonders of the Lord?
Let us open our eyes, our ears, and our hearts;
It is Christ the Lord.
It is He!

(Pat Uhl)

Reviewing Part Four

Summary

In this Part, you have learned several truths about your Catholic Faith.

1. The followers of Jesus form one living Body—the Mystical Body of Christ.
2. The Body of Christ is nourished and strengthened at the Eucharist.
3. Baptism, Confirmation, and Eucharist are the sacraments of Christian initiation. Christian initiation is a process of learning what it means to follow Jesus and to act as a Christian.
4. The sacrament of Holy Orders celebrates the fact that God calls some Christians to special ministries in the Body of Christ—the ministries of bishop, priest, and deacon.
5. By Baptism and Confirmation, all Christians are called to serve the needs of others.
6. The sacraments of Reconciliation and Anointing of the Sick are special signs of Christian healing for the spirit and the body.
7. The sacrament of Marriage celebrates the vocation people have to follow Jesus in the family unit. It is a sacrament in which a man and a woman pledge their love, respect, honor, and faithfulness for life.
8. Prayer is communication with God. Prayer is also part of a Christian's identity.

Questions

1. How did Saint Paul explain the Church to the people of Corinth?
2. Why is the Body of Christ sometimes called a Eucharistic community?
3. What are the four steps in the Rite of Christian Initiation?
4. What are the sacraments of initiation?
5. What are the sacraments of ministry?
6. What are the three steps in the process of healing?
7. In what ways are members of the Body of Christ called to be healers?
8. What are two purposes of marriage?
9. What is prayer?
10. What is one of the best ways to learn more about prayer?

True or False

Circle the T if the statement is true. Circle the F if the statement is false.

1. The sharing you do at Mass strengthens your membership in the Body of Christ.   T   F
2. Jesus said that everyone needs to be born again through a confession of sins and penance.   T   F
3. Becoming a member of the Body of Christ is a step-by-step process.   T   F
4. The order of deacon is not a sacrament.   T   F
5. Every member of the Body of Christ has a call to serve others.   T   F
6. It takes time, patience, and rest for healing to happen.   T   F

7. Anointing of the Sick is only for the health of the body.   T   F

8. Faithfulness is a very important family skill.   T   F

9. The support of the whole community is very important for the success of a marriage.   T   F

10. The most important attitude you can have about prayer is that of talking with a Friend.   T   F

Matching

Match the statement in column B which best fits each person in column A.

A

1. ___ Nicodemus
2. ___ The disciples of John
3. ___ Saint Paul
4. ___ Mother Teresa
5. ___ Father Solanus
6. ___ The Blessed Mother
7. ___ Dominic Savio
8. ___ Saint Dismas

B

a. "Do whatever He tells you."

b. "Jesus, remember me."

c. "You must be born again of water and the Spirit."

d. "I am talking with my Friend."

e. "Tell him that the blind see, the cripples walk, and the poor hear the Gospel."

f. "The love of God and the power of His Word healed her."

g. "Sister Anna, I'd like you to meet Jesus."

h. "The Body is one and has many members."

Vocabulary

Use each of the following terms in a sentence.

election	Viaticum
twelve tribes	tonsure
Holy Orders	schism
contrition	Sanhedrin

Celebration

Plan a special prayer service, penance service, or a class Mass as a special end-of-the-year event. Use prayers, readings, and ideas from the whole book. Set aside a special time for your celebration. You may wish to invite your parents or other guests. Remember, your celebration should express how proud and happy you are to be a follower of Jesus Christ and a member of His Body, the Church. Pages 284–285 of your Handbook will help you with your plans. Be sure to include music and actions.

Shout joyfully to God, all you on earth,
Sing praise to the glory of His name;
proclaim His glorious praise.

(Psalm 66:1)

Handbook

Glossary

You are learning many new words in religion class. These words help you understand what the People of God believe and teach. This glossary will help you with these words. Some of the words in this glossary you will already know. But they are repeated here to help you review what these words mean.

Absolution   The prayer that the priest says to show that God has forgiven a person's sins in the sacrament of Forgiveness. The word comes from a word that means "to wash." The prayer of absolution shows that sin has been washed away.

Addiction   The mental or physical need for some substance. A person who needs drugs or alcohol is said to suffer from drug or alcohol addiction.

Adoration   Prayer that tells God how much you love Him and His goodness. You simply talk with Jesus as you would talk with a friend.

Adultery   An act of unfaithfulness on the part of a husband or wife. Adultery is a very serious sin against the Law of God and the laws of the Church.

Agape   A friendly meeting, as in the meals eaten together by the early Christians. *Agape* comes from the Greek word meaning "love feast."

Anointing of the Sick   One of the seven sacraments of the Church. It is the sacrament of physical and spiritual healing for people who are sick or depressed. This sacrament is the way the people of a parish show their love for sick people and pray that they will get better.

Apostolicity   That sign which points to the beginning of the Church with the Apostles at Pentecost and to the Church's faithfulness to the teachings of the Apostles.

Baptism   One of the seven sacraments. It is the sacrament of new life given to people by Jesus. This sacrament is one of the sacraments of initiation.

Beatitudes   Short sayings that Jesus told the people in His Sermon on the Mount. The word comes from the first word in each saying. The word means "blessed" or "happy."

Bishop   The leader of the Catholics in a group of parishes called a diocese. The bishop has received the sacrament of Holy Orders.

Canonize   Officially calling a person a saint. A saint is canonized only after the Church studies the person's life on earth.

Capuchins   A branch of the Franciscan order. The Capuchins were founded by Brother Matthew of Urbano in 1525. Their name comes from the pointed hood, or capuche, worn by members of the order.

Catechumenate   The time a new Christian spends going through the steps of initiation. The period of time and the program of studies that a person follows while receiving the sacraments of initiation are called his or her catechumenate.

Chancellor   A person who assists the bishop in the running of a diocese. The chancellor helps carry on the business side of caring for the Catholics in a specific area.

Church   The People of God who believe in and follow Jesus. The Church is both an international organization of believers and the simple gathering of members of God's Family.

Cloister   A special place in the houses of religious men and women which is closed to outsiders. Cloisters provide the privacy sisters and brothers need for prayer and study.

Communion of Saints   Another name for the Family of God. The name shows that everyone who is baptized and who follows Jesus is a member of a Family that lasts even after a person dies.

Community   A group of people who share something in common. Your family is a community because you are all related to one another. Your school is a community because you are all going there to learn and to grow. Your parish is a community because you all believe in and follow Jesus.

Confirmation   One of the seven sacraments of the Church. It is the sacrament that gives Catholics the Holy Spirit to help them serve other people. Confirmation is one of the sacraments of initiation.

Consecrate   To make holy. When the priest consecrates the bread and wine at Mass, they become the Body and Blood of Christ.

Contrition   Sorrow for one's sins. Catholics say a prayer of contrition during the celebration of the sacrament of Reconciliation.

Council   A meeting of the pope and bishops to discuss Church teaching. From 1962 to 1964, the last council of the Church was held in Rome. It was called Vatican Council II.

Covenant   A bargain, an agreement, a special loving contract. God's covenant with His People was an agreement that He would be with His People and they would follow His Law.

Deacon   A person who has received the sacrament of Holy Orders. A deacon serves the Church by assisting the priest, preaching the Gospel, distributing Holy Communion, administering some of the sacraments, and visiting the sick.

Diocese   A specific area in the Church usually under the leadership of a bishop. A diocese includes all the Catholic people and parishes in the area.

Doctor of the Church   A title given to saints whose writing or preaching is helpful for Christians of all times and places. There are thirty-two doctors of the Church.

Election   The step in Christian initiation when the new member is chosen to receive the sacraments of Baptism, Confirmation, and First Eucharist.

Encyclical A letter written by the pope to bishops all around the world. Encyclicals teach many truths of the Catholic Faith and encourage people to stay faithful to God.

Ethics The study of behavior which shows the difference between right and wrong. Christian ethics is sometimes called morality.

Eucharist One of the seven sacraments of the Church. It is the sacrament of the Body and Blood of Jesus Christ. Catholics call the celebration of the Eucharist the Mass. The Eucharist is also one of the sacraments of initiation.

Evangelist A term for the authors of the four Gospels. The word *evangelist* means "a bearer of good news."

Gentiles A term used to indicate all non-Jewish peoples. Saint Paul, who preached mainly to non-Jews, became known as the Apostle of the Gentiles.

Grace A share in God's life, friendship with God. *Grace* is also the word used to talk about how God helps His People.

Habit The special clothing worn by members of religious orders. Dominicans wear a white habit with a black cape.

Holy Orders One of the seven sacraments of the Church. It is the sacrament of service and leadership for people who want to devote their entire lives to the preaching of the Gospel and to the nourishing of God's Family. The three orders are deacon, priest, and bishop.

Homage An act by which a person shows that he or she is willing to obey God's laws. Catholics pay homage to God at Mass.

Hypostatic union The term which is used to express the fact that Jesus is both human and divine. The hypostatic union means that the one Person of Jesus Christ has two separate natures.

Immaculate Conception A title given to Mary, meaning that from the beginning of her life, she was free from sin.

Incarnation The teaching of the Church that God became man in Jesus. The birth of Jesus is sometimes called the mystery of the Incarnation.

Infallibility The teaching of the Catholic Church that the Holy Spirit will help the pope and the bishops, when they join the pope, from being wrong when they teach about faith or morals. The pope is infallible when he speaks out as the representative of Jesus Christ on matters of faith.

Inspiration A term used to describe how the Holy Spirit helped the writers of the Bible to write what is true. The writers worked under the guidance, or inspiration, of the Holy Spirit.

Kerygma The Good News of salvation. The word *kerygma* means "good news." The teaching of the Apostles after Pentecost is called the kerygma.

Kingdom of God A term Jesus used when He was talking about the People of God—the Church. The term is sometimes used to mean heaven, too.

Land of Promise   Israel, the place that God promised to His People when He led them out of Egypt.

Liturgy   Another name for the Mass and the sacraments. Liturgy means the public prayer of the people who follow Jesus.

Marriage   One of the seven sacraments of the Church. It is the sacrament of love and faith for a man and woman who want to devote their entire lives to each other and to their children.

Messiah   The Chosen One of God, the person picked by God to help the people of Israel live the way God wanted them to live. Christians have always believed that Jesus is the Messiah.

Ministry   Another word for service. People who help others in the Family of God are said to have a ministry—a special call to serve others in some way.

Mission   A task a person is sent to accomplish. The mission of Jesus was to save the world from sin and death, and to announce the kingdom of God. The mission of baptized Christians is to continue the work of Jesus.

Morality   Individual and social behavior based on the Law and will of God. A person who obeys God's Law is said to have good morals, or morality.

Mystagogia   A time of special celebration and instruction for a newly baptized Catholic. The word *mystagogia* means "sharing the mysteries."

Mystery   A truth that can be known only after God reveals it but which still is impossible to understand completely.

The fact that Jesus is both God and human is a mystery.

Office   The Liturgy of the Hours, or formal prayer recited each day by priests, religious, and many lay people. The prayers for the Divine Office are found in the breviary.

Original sin   The first sin, the sin of Adam and Eve. Original sin describes the pull everyone feels toward doing things that are wrong.

Orthodox   Eastern Christian Churches which have their own special worship and tradition but are separated from the pope. The word *orthodox* means "true believing."

Paraclete   A title for the Holy Spirit. The word *paraclete* means "special helper."

Parousia   The final way Jesus will show Himself at the end of time when the kingdom of God is completed. It is also called the Second Coming.

Passover   The feast of the Jews that remembers the time God led His People out of Egypt. Jewish people celebrate this feast every year in March or April. Sometimes, the death and resurrection of Jesus are called His Passover.

Patriarchates   Very important cities in the growth of the Christian Church. The bishops who are in charge of these cities are called patriarchs. Rome, Constantinople, Alexandria, Jerusalem, and Antioch are patriarchates.

Pharisee   A class of Jewish leaders. They were the wise teachers of the Law of Moses. During the time of Jesus, some

Pharisees taught that obedience to the Law was more important than anything. Jesus reminded the Pharisees that love was the most important law.

Piety A gift of the Holy Spirit which helps people worship God. Praying is sometimes called an act of piety.

Priest A person who has received the sacrament of Holy Orders. The priest gives his life to serving God by being a leader and servant of the people who follow Jesus. The priest preaches and celebrates Mass and the sacraments. He also helps and cares for God's People.

Proverbs Short sayings about how the People of God should live. Jesus often used proverbs to teach the Good News of the kingdom of God.

Psalms Special prayers and poems found in the Bible. Some psalms express praise and thanks to God. Other psalms talk about fear or sorrow. They were originally hymns sung by the Israelites.

Reconciliation One of the seven sacraments of the Church. It is sometimes called confession, Forgiveness, or Penance. This sacrament is the way God has chosen to forgive people's sins and to bring them back into His Family.

Religious vows Public promises made to God. People who have a vocation to religious life make vows of poverty, chastity, and obedience.

Responsibility Being answerable for one's thoughts, words, and actions. People who try to follow the laws of God and the Church are showing Christian responsibility.

Reveal To make something known. God's plans for caring for His People were revealed to Abraham, Moses, and the prophets. Jesus reveals God the Father in Person.

Rite A set of traditions and customs that people use when they celebrate Mass and the sacraments. The Church celebrates Mass in different rites because the People of God have different traditions and customs.

Sabbath The seventh day of the week. The Jewish people set aside the Sabbath for prayer and worship.

Sacrament A special sign of God's love and grace. Jesus gave His People seven sacraments to help them grow: Baptism, Reconciliation, Eucharist, Confirmation, Anointing of the Sick, Marriage, and Holy Orders.

Sacrifice A solemn religious action in which something is offered to God. This is usually done by a priest representing the people. The Mass is the perfect sacrifice, offering Christ and the people with Him.

Sadducees A class of Jewish leaders. They were well educated and very traditional in religious matters. They did not accept any part of Jewish teaching that was not written in the Torah.

Sanhedrin A Jewish court at the time of Jesus. The Sanhedrin answered questions about Jewish law.

Schism A separation or a division in the Church. A schism is caused when groups in the Church have a serious disagreement and cannot settle it.

Seder Meal The sacred meal the Jewish people eat on the feast of Passover. There are special prayers and actions that are a part of this meal. Jesus ate the Seder Meal with His Apostles.

Sin Turning away from God, refusing to accept His love. Sin can be something wrong you do that hurts yourself or other people. It can also be something good that you refuse to do for yourself or other people. Serious sins are called mortal sins. Less serious sins are called venial sins.

Synods Meetings of members of the Church at which matters of teaching and behavior are discussed.

Synoptic Holding the same or a similar view. The Gospels of Matthew, Mark, and Luke are called synoptic because they follow the same general outline.

Theologian A person who studies and teaches about God. Theologians have a special vocation to help the followers of Jesus learn more about God, the Church, and the beliefs of the Family of God.

Third order A special way for lay people to be a part of the work and spirit of a religious order without becoming sisters or brothers. Members of third orders say special prayers and follow certain rules. The Franciscans, Dominicans, Carmelites, and others have third orders.

Tonsure The ancient ceremony by which a person became a member of the clergy. During tonsure, a lock of hair was cut from the crown of a person's head. The word *tonsure* means "haircut."

Torah The first five books of the Hebrew Scripture—Genesis, Exodus, Leviticus, Numbers, and Deuteronomy. The Torah is also known as the Books of the Law or the Pentateuch.

Twelve tribes The twelve divisions in the kingdom of Israel. Each of the twelve tribes was named for one of Jacob's sons. Another name for Jacob was Israel.

Viaticum The sacrament of the dying. When a person is dying, he or she is given the sacrament of Holy Communion, and special prayers are said. The word *viaticum* means "food for the journey."

Vices and virtues Vices are bad habits of acting, and virtues are good habits of acting. Avoiding vices and practicing virtue makes people stronger in their faith.

Vocation A special call from God to follow Him in a certain way. Marriage, Holy Orders, belonging to a religious order, and living as a single person are some examples of Christian vocations.

Wisdom literature The books of the Bible which give advice on how to live. The seven wisdom books are Job, Psalms, Proverbs, Ecclesiastes, Song of Songs, Wisdom, and Sirach.

Worship To pray, to celebrate liturgy, and to honor God. When you participate at Mass or do a kind deed because you love God, you are worshiping Him.

Seasons and Feasts

Glory to God

People throughout the world have searched for different ways to celebrate the meaning of Christ's birth. Carols, plays, festivals of light, and Christmas trees all symbolize the spirit of the birth and life of Jesus. Different countries have their own unique customs. Sometimes they adapt ancient rites and traditions to express their faith in Christmas.

All the various Christmas rituals proclaim the same message: "Glory to God in the highest, and on earth, peace to people of good will." All the rituals and celebrations try to spread a message of faith, hope, love, and happiness in a troubled world.

The word *carol* originally meant "dance," or "ring dance." People would gather in circles to dance and sing. Later, carols were those songs that were especially sung at Christmas time. They became the songs that reminded people about the birth of Jesus.

The first Christmas carol was probably written by Saint Francis of Assisi. His happy carol to the Infant Jesus became very popular in Italy. Carols soon spread to England, Ireland, France, Germany, and Spain. Throughout the world, the Christmas season has more songs, or carols, than any other religious or civil holiday.

Light of the World

Lighting fires and candles at midwinter was a meaningful ritual in the cold climates of Europe long before any Christian influence touched the custom. The flames symbolized the return of the sun.

Light is also a very important Christian symbol. The prophet Isaiah used the light symbol to remind Israel of its promised salvation. For two thousand years, Christians have called Jesus the Light of the World.

On Christmas Eve in Ireland, families decorate their windows with holly. The green holly in the dead of winter reminds the Irish of the Christian belief in life everlasting. In the center of the window, a candle glows in order to light the way for Mary and Joseph. Traditionally, the youngest child in the family lights the candle, and the rest of the family prays for the safety of all travelers.

In England, a huge log, called a yule log, is burned through Christmas Eve and all day on Christmas. This log is a sign that the coming of Jesus brought warmth to a world that had grown very cold. The light of candles and fires are important parts of Christmas celebrations because Jesus the "light has come, and the glory of the Lord shines" (Isaiah 60:1).

Carnival

The most important part of the Church Year is the celebration of Easter. Down through the ages, people have invented many ways to prepare for Easter and to celebrate the feast itself. Very early in the tradition of the Church, people set aside a special time of penance before Easter. This time of penance was based on the story of Jesus fasting for forty days in the desert.

This period of fasting usually meant giving up food and treats. People would eat only one small meal a day. This meal was called a collation. Because the forty days of Lent were so difficult, many people declared the period just before Lent to be a time of special feasting. This time is called carnival.

The Thursday before Ash Wednesday was the beginning of carnival. The word *carnival* comes from two Latin words which mean "good-bye meat." For the whole week before Lent, people used up all the rich foods they had in their cupboards. For this reason, the last day before Lent was often called "Fat Tuesday." In French, the words *Fat Tuesday* are *Mardi Gras*. In New Orleans and in Rio de Janeiro, there are still great carnivals, or Mardi Gras.

During carnival time in England, the people slice meat into egg shapes and fry them in butter. They call these treats collops. In Scotland, families make crowdie, a porridge cooked with butter and milk. These countries celebrate the Tuesday before Lent by eating pancakes.

Germans and Austrians make rich pasteries for Fat Tuesday. The Norwegians fill their everyday muffins with whipped cream and top them with frosting. All this feasting makes people more ready to give up some of the pleasures of living in order to be more ready for the great feast of Easter.

Lent

Lent begins with the reception of ashes on Ash Wednesday. The ashes are reminders of death. While in the past Lent has meant doing a lot of bodily penances, the Church now wants all Catholics to focus on changing their hearts.

Lent is the time of salvation. It is a time for reviewing what is expected of members of the Body of Christ and working harder to think, act, and believe like good members of the Body.

The fourth Sunday of Lent is called Laetare Sunday. The word *laetare* means "rejoice." It used to be the first word of the Mass for that day. The Church has a special celebration of joy on the fourth Sunday of Lent to remind all Catholics that the time of waiting is almost over. Any day now, the feast of Easter will arrive.

In England, Laetare Sunday became known as "Mothering Sunday." People who lived away from home baked special cakes and took them home to their mothers. Many homilies on Laetare Sunday are about Mary, the Mother of Jesus.

Holy Week

People in the early Church celebrated Palm Sunday by reenacting the entry of Jesus into Jerusalem. In early times, priests and lay people carried branches of palm, willow, olive, or spruce. They would walk from some meeting place in the town to the village church. Mass would be celebrated when the procession was over.

In the Middle Ages, the procession remained in the churchyard. A crucifix was decorated with flowers. At the end of the procession, the priests would sing hymns and chant blessings. Families would then go to the church cemetery to pray for the dead of the parish.

Today, Christians receive palms. They listen to the reading of the Gospel about Jesus entering Jerusalem. Then, they have some kind of procession. It can be very simple or very elaborate depending on local customs.

On Holy Thursday, Christians everywhere remember the Last Supper of Jesus. Catholics celebrate three very important realities on that day.

1. *The beginning of the priesthood.* The bishop usually has a special Mass with his priests. At this Mass, the holy oils are blessed. This Mass is called the Mass of the Chrism (the name of one of the holy oils). This Mass is celebrated only in the cathedral.

2. *The new commandment of love.* This reality is celebrated by reenacting the washing of the feet which Jesus did at the Last Supper. Most parishes also sing songs and say prayers which will remind everyone of the new commandment of love.

3. *The gift of the Eucharist.* Throughout the Mass for Holy Thursday, there are reminders of the great gift of the Eucharist. The joy and wonder of the Holy Thursday Mass show how happy Catholics are that Jesus is with them always in the Blessed Sacrament.

Easter

In the past, on Easter Eve, the followers of Jesus would become very joyful as soon as night fell. Every family would light every candle in the house until whole towns and villages radiated the expectation of the resurrection.

In Europe, Holy Saturday is a time for making Easter foods, especially the many kinds of bread and pastry which are part of the Easter feast. Most countries also have the custom of coloring and decorating eggs on that day.

Most Easter breads are sweet. They are made with honey, sugar, raisins, and nuts. In Russia, the bread is called *kulitch*. It is baked in tall baking tins which make it look like the onion-domed towers of the Russian churches. On top of the bread are molded the letters *X* and *V*. They stand for *Xristos Voskrese*, which means "Christ is risen!" In Austria, the shape of a lamb is imprinted on the Easter bread. In Italy, the bread is baked in the shape of a lamb.

Catholic Heritage

A Life of Jesus

It is important for every Catholic to know well the important events in the life of Jesus. The list of events given below comes from the Gospels and from what is known of Jewish society at the time when Jesus lived.

Early Life

—Jesus was born in Bethlehem sometime before Herod the Great, the king of Palestine, died in 4 B.C.
—He grew up in Nazareth in the province of Galilee.
—Jesus lived with Mary, His mother, and with Joseph, Mary's husband.
—Some of the close relatives of Jesus were James, Joseph, Simon, and Jude.
—Jesus spoke Aramaic—the everyday language of the Jews.
—Jesus could read and speak Hebrew—the language of the Bible.
—He had the normal schooling and training every young Jewish boy received.

Public Life

—When Jesus was about thirty years old, He was baptized by John the Baptizer. John was His cousin.
—Jesus did not join John. He began preaching and teaching on His own.
—Jesus taught in the synagogues, gathered followers, and taught those followers His Way.
—He associated with all kinds of people, including those which other teachers of His day ignored—public sinners, tax collectors, women and children, the poor, and the people who did not know the Law of Moses.
—Jesus lived the very difficult life of a traveling preacher.
—Jesus cured the sick, forgave sins, brought the dead back to life, and cast out evil spirits.
—Jesus did not join any political party. But because He was teaching about the need to change and to follow God in the heart, He did make enemies.
—The preaching, traveling, teaching, and wonder-working of Jesus lasted from three to four years.

The Final Journey

—Jesus entered Jerusalem with His followers as a very popular teacher.
—Jesus challenged the keepers of the Temple which made them very angry.
—The Temple authorities talked one of Jesus' own followers, Judas, into betraying Him.
—Jesus ate a Last Supper with His friends. There, He gave them the gift of the Holy Eucharist.
—That same evening, while Jesus was praying in the Garden of Gethsemane, Judas came with the soldiers of the Temple, and these soldiers arrested Jesus.

—That same night, Jesus was put to trial and found guilty of claiming to be God.

—Jesus was turned over to Roman authorities to be crucified.

—He died on a Friday afternoon. He was buried right away to make sure that He was in the tomb before the beginning of the Jewish Sabbath.

—On Sunday morning, Jesus rose from the dead. His followers found the tomb empty. They were frightened.

The Witnesses

—Jesus made several appearances to Mary, to the disciples on the road to Emmaus, and to the Apostles. He asked His followers to spread His teachings to the very ends of the earth.

—After a time, Jesus returned to His Father in heaven. This return is called His ascension.

—After Jesus returned to the Father, the Apostles waited and prayed in a room in the city of Jerusalem.

—After ten days, the Holy Spirit came to the Apostles. The Spirit filled them with understanding and courage.

—At once, they began to teach about the life, death, and resurrection of Jesus.

—On the day the Spirit came, the Apostles baptized over three thousand people.

The Basic Catholic Teachings

Your first introduction to faith came when you were baptized, probably as an infant. You spent many years after that time learning and growing. You made your First Communion and joined a community which celebrated that learning and growing in the Eucharist. In receiving the sacrament of Confirmation, you look deeper into your faith. You try to understand for yourself the promises your parents and godparents made for you at your baptism.

But it doesn't stop there. The sacraments give you special helps, or graces, to assist you on your journey of faith. They don't make you a believer instantly or magically. Through your whole life, there will be times when believing is difficult—times when you need to ask questions or to challenge what other people tell you. This is natural.

Fortunately, you don't have to make the journey of faith all by yourself. The whole Church travels together. The members of your family, your teachers, your friends, your parish community—all these people can help you to grow as a believer. And you have four special helps, too: prayer, the liturgy, Scripture, and tradition.

1. *Prayer.* When you communicate with God, you are praying. When you pray with other people—your family, your classmates, your parish—you can feel a sense of community that is the Church, the People of God.

2. *The Liturgy.* The public prayer of the Church—most especially the Mass—is called the liturgy. For the growing believer, the Eucharistic liturgy is many things. It is a reminder of the greatest event of faith: the life, death, and resurrection of Jesus. It is a joyful celebration of community and a family meal. Through the readings, prayers, and homily, the Mass becomes a place to learn and to grow in faith.

3. *Scripture.* All of the things Catholics believe have their roots in Scripture. That is why reading the Bible should be a part of any believer's life. The Bible is the Word of God to His People, all of His People. When you take time to read and to think about the Scriptures, or to study them together in class, you will find a very simple message that has meaning for all time. You should have your own copy of the Bible. Then, you can explore the Word of God at your own pace. Throughout your life, you can turn to the Scriptures for wisdom, inspiration, and comfort.

4. *Tradition.* Out of the basic messages of the Good News has grown a body of knowledge called tradition—the way the official teachers of the Church have interpreted the Word of God. It is the collected wisdom of the Church, the continuing search for understanding and belief. This is your heritage as a member of the People of God.

What follows now is a summary of what Catholics believe. Reflect on these beliefs through prayer, liturgy, and Scripture.

The Holy Trinity—the Mystery of the One God

The history of salvation is the story of God's relationship with His People. Through it, God reveals Himself in Three Persons—Father, Son, and Holy Spirit—and saves His People from sin. The mystery of Three Persons in One God is called the Holy Trinity.

Belief in the Holy Trinity is at the heart of the Catholic Faith. Catholics are called to a lifelong, growing relationship with the Three Divine Persons. The people celebrate this mystery of God's love present in the world.

God the Father

From the beginning of time, God has revealed Himself to His People as a loving Father. He created the whole universe out of His love. He gives each person the gift of life. In every age, God has continued His loving relationship with His People, freeing them and saving them. God's saving love was actively shown in the history of Israel. It came to fulfillment in the life, death, and resurrection of Jesus. And it is still present today, as it will be for all generations, calling everyone into His kingdom.

Jesus, the Savior Lord

The greatest of all God's works is the Incarnation—the taking on of human flesh by His own Son, Jesus Christ. God loves His People so much that He became one of them, in the Person of Jesus. Jesus is the Messiah, the Savior, who was promised by God from the beginning of time. Through His birth, He proclaimed a new creation. In His life and teachings, Jesus showed how to live as children of the Father.

Jesus suffered and died so that all people might be freed from the sins that keep them from being fully human. In dying, Jesus destroyed death. Jesus rose from the dead and showed that life in God's love never really ends. The resurrection of Jesus is the central truth of the Catholic Faith. The reality of the resurrection transforms the whole world. Catholics celebrate the death and resurrection of Jesus and His presence in the Eucharist.

The Holy Spirit, the Comforter

The Holy Spirit, the Third Person of the Blessed Trinity, is the living gift of the Father's love, sent through Jesus into the world. At the Last Supper, Jesus promised that God would send the Spirit of Truth, the Comforter, to the Apostles. And on the feast of Pentecost, when the Apostles were gathered fearfully behind locked doors, the Spirit came upon them, symbolized by wind and flames. Filled with the Holy Spirit, the Apostles went forth to preach the Good News of Jesus. That day, the Church began to spread.

The Holy Spirit works in the Church. The gift of the Spirit, received in the sacrament of Confirmation, strengthens God's People for the journey of faith. It is through the grace of the Holy Spirit that the community of Christian believers has remained a vital presence in the world.

The Church, the People of God

The Church was founded by Jesus through His death and resurrection. At Pentecost, the Church received the gift of the Holy Spirit. The Catholic Church today carries on the tradition of faith, the sacraments, and the ministry of the first Apostles. Through these gifts, the Church continues to grow as a community of believers and a sign of God's love.

The Church is a community with Christ as its Head. Every member of the Church is called to proclaim the Good News. In this work, the Church is directed by its leaders, the Holy Father and the bishops.

The Sacraments, Signs of God's Love

The Church is a special sign of God's love. Within the Church, there are other signs, other ways in which God's love is seen and celebrated. These signs are the sacraments. They are Jesus' gifts to the Church. Although the Church administers the sacraments, they are signs of the presence of Jesus. In the sacraments, God's love in Christ comes face-to-face with the faith of the people.

The seven sacraments are Baptism, Confirmation, Eucharist, Reconciliation, Anointing of the Sick, Marriage, and Holy Orders. These sacraments are sources of God's grace—moments throughout life when people are given the opportunity to grow in faith. The sacraments are moments of shared memory and celebration.

God's Law

Every day people face countless choices between right and wrong. Their choices are based on their values—the things they believe and cherish. The Christian's value system is based on God's unchanging Law as revealed in the Ten Commandments and later—through Jesus—in the Beatitudes. Whenever a Christian makes choices which go against these values, he or she experiences the brokenness and lack of freedom that is sin.

In making choices, the Christian is guided by the Word of God, by the collective wisdom of the Church, and by the good example of members of the community. But the Christian also has an individual conscience given by God and sustained by the Holy Spirit. Consciences are formed through a whole lifetime of living in God's Law and in His love.

Christian Life

Beyond personal morality, Christians have a mission to the whole world. No Christian lives in isolation. The Christian has a responsibility to make God's kingdom of justice and peace a reality in the world. It is not enough just to hear God's Word—the Christian has to live it.

From the very beginning, the sign which marked all Christians was their great love. At many times throughout history, that love conflicted with civil laws. Christians triumphed. Christian witness and service are very difficult ideals in any time, but the reward—the building of God's kingdom—is great.

Mary and the Saints

Christians are not alone on the journey of faith. They can look ahead to the people who have gone before, Christians in past times whose lives were models for all believers. The Church celebrates these people, or saints, because they were real human beings who went through the same struggles all people do and who perservered.

The first among all these special people is Mary, the Mother of God. Catholics recognize that Mary was a human being who is special because she brought Jesus into the world and continues to bring Him closer to His People.

The Final Reunion

Catholics believe in a life after death. The quality of life after death is determined by a person's response to God's love here on earth. If the response has been open and loving, if the person has sincerely tried to live as Jesus did, then he or she will be welcomed into God's kingdom called heaven. If the response has been less than loving, if there are still things to work on, the person will experience a time of probation, of further growth called purgatory. Those who die consciously rejecting God's love will experience the absence of that love, called hell.

Christians also believe that at some point, the process of creation will come to an end. This will happen only when all creation has reached its fullest potential. Then, the kingdom of God will come at last.

Prayers and Actions

How to Make Up Your Own Prayer

When you write a prayer, you can use an outline to help you. Follow these four simple steps in writing prayers.

1. *Greeting.* For example, "Dear Jesus" or "Heavenly Father" or "Most Blessed Virgin Mary" or "Dear Saint Francis."

2. *Remember.* Remember an event and thank the person. For example, if you are addressing Jesus, "Thank You for dying on the cross for me and for giving me a new life through Your resurrection."

3. *Ask.* Ask for help. For example, "Please help me to follow You today by saying something kind to someone," or "Help me to obey my parents and teachers."

4. *Praise.* Praise God and offer Him worship. For example, "I ask this through Jesus Christ, who lives and reigns forever and ever. Amen."

How to Plan a Prayer Service

1. *Choose a theme.* You must decide what it is you are celebrating. It may be Mary's love or the Ten Commandments. A theme can be anything you want to celebrate.

2. *Choose music.* Plan to sing two or three songs during the prayer service. The songs may be in music books or on record albums that you can play.

3. *Choose Scripture.* Plan to read one or two passages from the Bible.

4. *Choose prayers and actions.* Pick prayers to say, or write your own. If there are going to be any special actions, write them, too.

Simple Prayer Service

Theme _____
Materials needed _____
Readings, if any _____
Responsibilities:
    Reader _____
    Song leader _____
    Prayer leader _____
Music, if any _____

Longer Prayer Service

Theme _____
Where _____
When _____
Atmosphere _____
1. Art and decorations _____
2. Music _____
3. Special action _____
Scripture:
    1. _____
    2. _____
    3. _____
Readers _____
_____

How to Plan a Eucharistic Celebration

Remember that when you prepare a Mass, you are helping people praise and worship the Father. The outline of the Mass given below will be a big help for you in your planning.

1. Introductory rites
   a. Entrance song
   b. Greeting
   c. Penitential rite
   d. Glory to God
   e. Opening prayer
2. Liturgy of the Word
   a. First reading (Old Testament) and response
   b. Second reading (New Testament) and response
   c. Third reading (Gospel) and response
   d. Homily
   e. Profession of Faith
   f. Prayer of the faithful
3. Liturgy of the Eucharist
   a. Preparation of the gifts
   b. Prayer over the gifts
   c. Eucharistic Prayer: preface, prayer, memorial acclamation, amen
   d. Communion: the Lord's Prayer, sign of peace, breaking of the Bread, Communion, song, prayer after Communion
   e. Concluding rite: greeting, blessing, dismissal

How to Go to Confession

How to confess. The following points describe how you go to confession.

1. The priest greets you.
2. The priest then says a short prayer to help you have trust in God. You respond, "Amen."
3. The priest may then read a selection from Scripture to help you think about God's love and forgiveness.
4. You tell your sins to the priest. He then talks with you on how to become a better Christian.
5. The priest then gives you a penance, something that you agree to do in order to help make up for your faults and sins.
6. The priest invites you to tell God how sorry you are by your saying an act of contrition.
7. Finally, the priest says the prayer of absolution: "God, the Father of mercies, through the death and resurrection of His Son, has reconciled the world to Himself and sent the Holy Spirit among us for forgiveness of sins; through the ministry of the Church, may God give you pardon and peace, and I absolve you from your sins in the name of the Father, and of the Son, and of the Holy Spirit." You reply, "Amen."
8. Right after the absolution, the priest says, "Give thanks to the Lord, for He is good." You reply, "His mercy endures forever."
9. The priest then says, "The Lord has freed you from your sins. Go in peace."

Traditional Prayers

The Lord's Prayer

Our Father, who art in heaven,
hallowed be Thy name.
Thy kingdom come; Thy will be done
on earth as it is in heaven.
Give us this day our daily bread,
and forgive us our trespasses
as we forgive those who trespass
against us.
And lead us not into temptation
but deliver us from evil.
Amen.

The Apostles' Creed

I believe in God, the Father almighty,
Creator of heaven and earth;
and in Jesus Christ, His only Son, our
Lord;
who was conceived by the Holy Spirit,
born of the Virgin Mary, suffered under
Pontius Pilate, was crucified, died, and
was buried.
He descended into hell;
the third day He arose again from the
dead;
He ascended into heaven, sits at the right
hand of God, the Father almighty;
from thence He shall come to judge the
living and the dead.
I believe in the Holy Spirit, the holy
Catholic Church, the communion of
saints, the forgiveness of sins, the
resurrection of the body, and life
everlasting.
Amen.

The Hail Mary

Hail, Mary, full of grace,
the Lord is with thee.
Blessed art thou among women,
and blessed is the Fruit
of thy womb, Jesus.
Holy Mary, Mother of God,
pray for us sinners, now,
and at the hour of death.
Amen.

Remember Prayer to Mary

Remember, O most gracious Virgin Mary,
that never was it known
that anyone who fled to thy protection,
implored thy help, or sought thine
intercession was left unaided.
Inspired with this confidence I fly
unto thee, O Virgin of Virgins,
my Mother.
To thee I come, before thee I stand
sinful and sorrowful.
O Mother of the Word Incarnate,
despise not my petitions but
in thy mercy hear and answer me.
Amen.

Act of Faith

O my God, I firmly believe that You are
one God in three Divine Persons: the
Father, the Son, and the Holy Spirit. I
believe in Jesus Christ, Your Son, who
became a Man and died for our sins, and
who will come to judge the living and
the dead. I believe these and all the
truths which the holy Catholic Church
teaches, because You who know all have
revealed them. Amen.

Act of Hope

O my God, trusting in Your goodness and promises, I hope to obtain pardon of my sins, the help of Your grace, and life everlasting, through the merits of Jesus Christ, my Lord and Redeemer. Amen.

Act of Love

O my God, I love You above all things, because You are all-good and worthy of my love. I love my neighbor as myself for love of You. I forgive all who have injured me, and I ask pardon for all whom I have injured. Amen.

A Prayer for Forgiveness

My God,
I am sorry for my sins with all my heart.
In choosing to do wrong
   and failing to do good,
I have sinned against You
   whom I should love above all things.
With Your help,
   I will do penance,
   sin no more,
   and avoid those things which lead me
     to make wrong choices.
Jesus Christ suffered and died for us.
In His name, dear Father, forgive me.

Glory Be to the Father

Glory be to the Father,
   and to the Son,
   and to the Holy Spirit.
As it was in the beginning,
   is now, and ever shall be,
   world without end.
Amen.

Lists Catholics Remember

The Ten Commandments

1. I am the Lord your God. You shall have no other gods besides Me.

2. You shall not take the name of the Lord, your God, in vain.

3. Remember to keep holy the Sabbath day.

4. Honor your mother and father.

5. You shall not murder.

6. You shall not commit adultery.

7. You shall not steal.

8. You shall not lie.

9. You shall not desire your neighbor's wife.

10. You shall not desire anything that belongs to your neighbor.

The Rules of the Church

1. Take part in the Eucharist every Sunday and holy day. Do no unnecessary work on Sunday.

2. Receive the sacraments frequently.

3. Study about the Good News of Jesus.

4. Follow the marriage laws of the Church.

5. Support the People of God.

6. Do penance on certain days.

7. Reach out to others. Support the missionary effort of the Church.

The Beatitudes

Blest are those lowly who seek God;
  the reign of God is theirs.
Blest are the sorrowing;
  they shall be consoled.
Blest are the lowly;
  they shall inherit the land.
Blest are they who hunger and thirst for
    what is right;
  they shall have their fill.
Blest are they who show mercy;
  mercy shall be theirs.
Blest are those who serve God with all
    their hearts;
  they shall see God.
Blest are the peacemakers;
  they shall be called the children of God.
Blest are those persecuted for doing the
    right thing;
  the reign of God is theirs.
        (Adapted from *Matthew 5:3–10*)

The Works of Mercy

For the Body
Feed the hungry.
Give drink to the thirsty.
Clothe the naked.
Shelter the homeless.
Visit the sick.
Visit the imprisoned.
Bury the dead.

For the Heart
Help the sinner.
Teach the ignorant.
Counsel the doubtful.
Comfort the sorrowful.
Bear wrongs patiently.
Forgive injuries.
Pray for the living and the dead.

The Seven Sacraments

Baptism
Confirmation
Eucharist
Penance, or Reconciliation
Anointing of the Sick
Holy Orders
Marriage

Special Holy Days

The Solemnity of Mary, Mother of God
  (January 1)
Ascension Thursday (Forty days after
  Easter)
The Feast of the Assumption of Mary
  (August 15)
All Saints' Day (November 1)
The Feast of the Immaculate Conception
  of Mary (December 8)
Christmas (December 25)

Special Penances

Not eating meat
Eating less
Giving up treats
Saying extra prayers
Being silent
Doing special kind deeds
Reading from the Bible
Attending the Eucharist on weekdays
Giving money to the poor or to special
  causes

Days of Penance

The days of Advent
Ash Wednesday
The days of Lent, especially Fridays